LIGHTHOUSE REVIEW

The Ultimate
Verbal and Vocabulary
Builder

Published by Lighthouse Review, Inc., Austin, Texas 78716

Lighthouse Review, Inc.
The Ultimate Verbal and Vocabulary Builder

ISBN: 0-9677594-1-2

CONTENTS

RELATED PUBLICATIONS

Are you or someone you know taking the LSAT, GRE, GMAT, or SAT? If so, check out the comprehensive review materials published by Lighthouse Review, Inc.

LSAT. The *Lighthouse LSAT Prep Self-Study Course* is a well organized, challenging study program which has been carefully designed to prepare students for the LSAT. The program is organized by question type. Each section contains detailed expository materials, summaries of important concepts and procedures and timed practice exercises. Detailed written explanations follow each exercise. The course includes an up-to-date 350 page textbook, two full, simulated LSATs, a complete study plan and access to our telephone help-line.

GRE. The *Lighthouse GRE Prep Self-Study Course* is a well organized, challenging study program which has been carefully designed to prepare students for the GRE. The program is organized by question type. Each section contains detailed expository materials, summaries of important concepts and procedures and timed practice exercises. Detailed written explanations follow each exercise.The course includes a 500 page textbook, our 250 page Ultimate Math Refresher workbook, this Ultimate Verbal and Vocabulary Builder workbook, a full, simulated GRE, a complete study plan and access to our telephone help-line.

GMAT. The *Lighthouse GMAT Prep Self-Study Course* is a well organized, challenging study program which has been carefully designed to prepare students for the GMAT. The program is organized by question type. Each section contains detailed expository materials, summaries of important concepts and procedures and timed practice exercises. Detailed written explanations follow each exercise. The course includes an up-to-date 500 page textbook, our 250 page Ultimate Math Refresher workbook, three full, simulated GMATs, a detailed step-by-step study plan and access to our telephone help-line.

SAT. The *Lighthouse SAT Prep Self-Study Course* stresses fundamentals and provides in-depth instruction that you can master at you own pace. Your SAT score is too important for you to walk into the test unprepared. SAT now stands for Scholastic Assessment Test. This change highlights the fact that the SAT is not a test of intelligence, but rather a test of skills. That's why Lighthouse provides techniques and skills exercises in a well organized, challenging study program.

The program is organized by question type. Each section contains detailed expository materials, summaries of important concepts and procedures and timed practice exercises. Detailed written explanations follow each exercise. The course includes a 500 page textbook, tour 250 page Ultimate Math Refresher workbook, this Ultimate Verbal and Vocabulary Builder workbook, a full, simulated SAT, a complete study plan and access to our telephone help-line.

To learn more information about our programs, go to our website at www.lighthousereview.com, drop us an e-mail at info@lighthousereview.com, call us at (512) 306-9701, send us a facsimile at (512) 328-4137, or write us at Lighthouse Review, Inc., P.O. Box 160205, Austin, Texas 78716-0205.

VOCABULARY REVIEW

Introduction

A person's vocabulary is not acquired overnight, or even over a weekend of intense study. It is accumulated over many years, and by a variety of methods. As children, we learn simple words expressing simple concepts. As adults, we become acquainted with more sophisticated language. The average adult has a vocabulary of about 30,000 words. A college senior or graduate will presumably have a much greater than average vocabulary (100,000 words is about the upper limit). The level of vocabulary tested is that of a college-educated adult. It presupposes, first of all, fluency in the English language. Some of the questions on the vocabulary portion of the test use idiomatic English, which can be extremely difficult for the non-native speaker of English. This book is intended to familiarize you with the kind of language you can expect to encounter. It has been sent to you in advance of our weekend seminar so that you may build your vocabulary in a meaningful way. Obviously, we do not have advance access to the words that will be on the test that you will take, but we have examined numerous past tests and picked out the most difficult words on these tests. We have compiled a list from this, and we have placed words that have frequently occurred at the beginning of the list.

The exercises in this book are **not** in test format. Your study manual will cover those formats in great detail. In this book we have devised a format that is specifically geared toward learning *new* vocabulary. We have relied on the most current research in the fields of cognitive science and educational psychology when creating this book[1]. The order of the exercises and the parts of the individual exercises are such that you will learn the greatest possible number of vocabulary words and retain these words in an effective manner. Additionally, you will be able to use this same format when you encounter unfamiliar words in everyday life.

---

[1]Blick, Kenneth A. and Dorothy A. Flannagan. "Levels of processing and the retention of word meanings." *Perceptual Motor Skills* 68 (1989): 1123-1128.

PART 1: HOW TO BUILD YOUR VOCABULARY

Methods

Reviewing lists of words and attempting to memorize their definitions (rote method) is not a very effective way of learning vocabulary. In fact, it is next to useless, yet many study books tell students to look at long lists of difficult words and try to remember the definitions. Study after study has shown that people build their vocabularies by reading, hearing, and using words IN CONTEXT. Very often, you can guess what a word means simply by knowing what the words surrounding it mean, and the way the word is used. Some recent studies have shown that when a student uses a new, unfamiliar word in such a way that it refers to the student herself or himself, that retention surpasses even the context method of vocabulary study. This is called 'self-reference' and researchers in the field of cognitive science believe that self-referential knowledge is more deeply ingrained in the mind than knowledge acquired by other methods. Specific studies testing vocabulary acquisition have shown that students who learn by more than one memory 'route' will retain and retrieve information better. What this means for you is that for each word in this book, you will be asked to write a sentence using that word in such a way that it pertains to you or does or does not describe you. You will be given some specific examples of this further along in the book.

The words we use in ordinary conversation are the words we know best. Often, when we encounter unknown words in textbooks, newspapers, and novels, we simply skim over them with a vague notion of 'looking them up later.' NOW IS THE TIME!!! Look those words up! Keep a dictionary by you when you read, so that you can look words up quickly and easily. By looking them up while you have your reading matter at hand, you will know the context of the word, and you will remember what it means later. If you cannot have a dictionary at hand, write down the unfamiliar word along with the sentence in which you found it. We have included some blank vocabulary exercise forms at the end of this book for you to photocopy and keep on hand for this purpose. Make a note of your new word. Use it in conversation and impress your friends ("My, what an adipose feline you have!"). The more you use words in context, the better you will remember them.

We have purposely not put the words in alphabetical order. Too many students find themselves adept at words beginning with A through D, and never get through a whole book. By having our exercises not in alphabetical order, you will learn a variety of words, even if you do not finish the entire book.

Tools

In addition to this Workbook, you will need to have at hand two books: a dictionary and a thesaurus. The dictionary should be any reputable, up-to-date dictionary (if you do not think being up-to-date is important, we suggest you look up the word 'computer' in a dictionary over twenty years old). Be careful about the kind of dictionary you are using. The *Oxford English Dictionary* is the definitive dictionary of the English language, however it is an historical dictionary and as such puts the oldest definition first. We recommend the Merriam-Webster *New Collegiate Dictionary*. It puts the primary, current meaning of the word first, and it gives some advice on usage. Also, you will need a thesaurus that is organized conceptually, not a dictionary-style thesaurus. These conceptual thesauri are usually called Roget's, since Peter Mark Roget developed this method of relating words according to ideas. This kind of thesaurus will allow you to see the relationships between words, as well as word opposites (antonyms). We recommend Harper & Row's *Roget's International Thesaurus*. If you already have a dictionary and thesaurus, do not feel obligated to go out and purchase the ones we recommend, but by all means use the tools you already have at your disposal.

Instructions

1. Read the word along with the brief definition provided. If you believe that you know the word already, then go on to the next word.

2. Read the context sentence.

3. Use your thesaurus to find two or three synonyms for the word. These should be words that you already know.

4. Using these words, try to come up with an appropriate antonym (opposite), if possible.

5. Write one or two sentences using the new word in a meaningful way.

6. Write one sentence showing how the word may or may not describe you or pertain to you in some way. Use first person ("I") in this sentence.

7. There will be quizzes throughout the book. After each quiz, take the words you got wrong and re-do the exercises, writing different sentences.

Here are some examples of self-referential statements:

untenable   To my chagrin, I discovered that my position in my argument with Harry was **untenable**.

verbose   I can be extremely **verbose** when I write on the subject of modern poetry.

adhere   My grandfather **adheres** strictly to the kosher laws, while I adhere only to the cultural artifacts of Judaism.

These sentences should be about **YOU**. Do not just make up any sentence and substitute "I" for another noun or pronoun. The point of the exercise is to connect the new word to some experience you have had, or some part of your definition of yourself. In this way, you will be able to retain the meaning of the word better than you might be able to otherwise.

Many words have more than one meaning. In general, we have chosen the most common meaning of a word, and have boiled it down to a brief phrase or one or two synonyms. Sometimes we have included two or even three definitions if the word is commonly used in all senses. You will recognize multiple definitions by a boldfaced 'or' between the definitions. In instances where there are two or more definitions, there will be as many context sentences given, *in the order that the definitions are given*. In other words, the first definition corresponds with the first context sentence. You should write full exercises for all definitions. In the quizzes, we will test only one definition.

After each definition, the part of speech of each word is indicated by an abbreviation. (adj) is adjective, (n) is noun, and (v) is verb. No other parts of speech are used in this book. The abbreviation 'esp.' is used occasionally in the definitions and means 'especially.'

Here is an example of a complete exercise. The portions which you will complete are in *italics*.

GREGARIOUS   outgoing, very friendly (adj)

Synonyms: *talkative, sociable*

Antonyms: *shy, reserved*

Context: Because Aileen is very **gregarious**, she would be the best person for the welcoming committee.

                   *Johnny is so **gregarious** that he will talk to anyone, even total strangers.*

Self-Referential: *I am not a **gregarious** person; usually I am a wall flower.*

PART 2: VOCABULARY BUILDING EXERCISES

INDIGENOUS native, originating in a place (adj)

Synonyms:

Antonyms:

Context: The **indigenous** peoples of South America are threatened by development in the rain forests.

Self-Referential:

SUBJECTIVE relating to the mind as the subject of experience (adj)

Synonyms:

Antonyms:

Context: Human emotions can only be experienced in a **subjective** manner; they are inexplicable to an outside observer.

Self-Referential:

PARADOX seeming contradiction **or** an actual contradiction(n)

Synonyms:

Antonyms:

Context: The **paradox** of time travel will be resolved when we learn more about the nature of space and time as a continuum.

  It is a **paradox** that while Dan speaks publicly about good parenting, at home he is distant and neglectful of his children.

Self-Referential:

ANOMALOUS irregular, unusual (adj)

Synonyms:

Antonyms:

Context: Darwin once said that there is nothing more **anomalous** in nature than a bird that cannot fly.

Self-Referential:

VISCOUS having a thick consistency, gelatinous (adj)

Synonyms:

Antonyms:

Context: Winnie discovered that the **viscous** fluid dripping from the kitchen cupboard was, in fact, honey oozing from a cracked jar.

Self-Referential:

EPHEMERAL fleeting, of short life or duration (adj)

Synonyms:

Antonyms:

Context: Sand castles are an **ephemeral** art form; they last only until the next tide.

Self-Referential:

CORROBORATE to confirm, to make certain (v)

Synonyms:

Antonyms:

Context: Ethel could not find a witness to **corroborate** her alibi, so she was convicted on all counts.

Self-Referential:

IMPLICIT implied, tacitly understood (adj)

Synonyms:

Antonyms:

Context: Many constitutional scholars believe that the right of privacy is **implicit** in the Bill of Rights, even though it is nowhere stated as such.

Self-Referential:

LUCID clear, understandable (adj)

Synonyms:

Antonyms:

Context: Teddy was surprisingly **lucid** after the car wreck; I know I would have been babbling nonsense.

Self-Referential:

PRODIGAL foolishly generous, not thrifty (adj)

Synonyms:

Antonyms:

Context: Katherine was being **prodigal** with her inheritance, instead of setting some of it aside for her old age.

Self-Referential:

FEIGN to pretend (v)

Synonyms:

Antonyms:

Context: Joe found it difficult to **feign** surprise when he had known all along what he was getting for Christmas.

Self-Referential:

SPECIOUS having the deceptive look of truth (adj)

Synonyms:

Antonyms:

Context: The Senator seems to prefer a **specious** argument to a sound one, and a plausible statement to a truthful one.

Self-Referential:

ARBITRARY   random, capricious, impartial (adj)

Synonyms:

Antonyms:

Context: Theresa's decision to cast Bob rather than Fred in the leading role
was purely **arbitrary**.

Self-Referential:

INTREPID   bold, fearless (adj)

Synonyms:

Antonyms:

Context: Sarah's **intrepid** plan to rescue the stranded hikers was frustrated by
overly cautious park officials.

Self-Referential:

ANTAGONISM   hostility, enmity (n)

Synonyms:

Antonyms:

Context: There was enormous **antagonism** between the Capulets and the
Montagues, resulting in great tragedy for their children.

Self-Referential:

ANTIPATHY   strong feeling against, dislike for (n)

Synonyms:

Antonyms:

Context: Despite the fact that his whole family loved it, George had great **antipathy** toward broccoli.

Self-Referential:

DOGMA   firmly held belief

Synonyms:

Antonyms:

Context: It is a **dogma** of academia that if one does not publish papers, then one does not merit tenure.

Self-Referential:

PERTINENT   clearly relevant (adj)

Synonyms:

Antonyms:

Context: Gerald's discourse on the mating habits of chimpanzees was not **pertinent** to the class on cellular biology.

Self-Referential:

VARIANCE   difference, disagreement (n)

Synonyms:

Antonyms:

Context: Meghan's interpretation of the events of last night is at **variance** with the accounts of her friends.

Self-Referential:

INCOMPATIBLE   not well matched, unsuited (adj)

Synonyms:

Antonyms:

Context: Because Albert smokes and Nell is a non-smoker, they are definitely **incompatible** as office-mates.

Self-Referential:

ISOLATE   to separate and make alone or single (v)

Synonyms:

Antonyms:

Context: Scientists in France and the United States vied to be the first to **isolate** the HIV virus.

Self-Referential:

SEVER   to cut off completely (v)

Synonyms:

Antonyms:

Context: The former junkie sought to **sever** his ties with his former friends who still used drugs.

Self-Referential:

SYNTHESIS   the combination of diverse elements into one (n)

Synonyms:

Antonyms:

Context: Walter's personality was a peculiar **synthesis** of flightiness and a great ability to concentrate on the task at hand.

Self-Referential:

ENGENDER   to create, foster (v)

Synonyms:

Antonyms:

Context: Marjorie did her best to **engender** feelings of goodwill and community among the members of the club.

Self-Referential:

DISCRETE   distinct, separate (adj)

Synonyms:

Antonyms:

Context: The Mathematics Department is a **discrete** entity, and is not part of the College of Science and Engineering.

Self-Referential:

PRACTICE SET 1

Instructions: Circle the answer that most closely approximates the definition of the word given.

1. **intrepid**   (A) silly   (B) clumsy   (C) bold   (D) fearful   (E) intricate

2. **dogma**   (A) ritual   (B) belief   (C) assumption   (D) slur   (E) dog-like

3. **paradox**   (A) contradiction   (B) model   (C) theoretical framework   (D) jumble   (E) point in time

4. **lucid**   (A) opaque   (B) leaf-like   (C) babbling   (D) clear   (E) slick

5. **prodigal**   (A) runaway   (B) poor   (C) wasteful   (D) biblical   (E) returning

6. **implicit**   (A) tacit   (B) overt   (C) blatant   (D) irregular   (E) untenable

7. **specious**   (A) tiny   (B) roomy   (C) grim   (D) apparently worthless   (E) seemingly true

8. **arbitrary**   (A) handy   (B) tasteful   (C) dramatic   (D) random   (E) contrary

9. **antipathy**   (A) pathetic   (B) appetizer   (C) dislike   (D) drunkenness   (E) parenthetical

10. **pertinent**   (A) sharp   (B) tined   (C) relevant   (D) beautiful   (E) unresolved

11. **discrete**   (A) separate   (B) modest   (C) confidential   (D) mathematical   (E) refined

12. **variance**   (A) permit   (B) difference   (C) curtain   (D) deviant   (E) varietal

13. **subjective**   (A) internal perception   (B) exterior view   (C) philosophical   (D) materially apparent   (E) empirical

14. **viscous**   (A) thick and gooey   (B) runny   (C) mean and rabid   (D) oily   (E) terrifying

15. **indigenous**   (A) birth defect   (B) primitive   (C) stone age   (D) native   (E) destitute

16. **incompatible**   (A) unaffectionate   (B) unfeeling   (C) not suited   (D) well-liked   (E) unfortunate

17. **anomalous**   (A) irregular   (B) wordy   (C) similar   (D) serrated   (E) blatant

18. **sever**   (A) harsh   (B) cut   (C) stern   (D) mince   (E) stew

19. **feign**   (A) pretend   (B) desire   (C) ruling   (D) govern   (E) become

20. **ephemeral**   (A) butterfly   (B) sandy   (C) gauzy   (D) fleeting   (E) of the night sky

21. **implicit**   (A) overt   (B) inherent   (C) compliant   (D) conspiratorial   (E) puckish

22. **isolate** (A) inhibit (B) refrigerate (C) cellular (D) separate (E) cold front

23. **engender** (A) sex (B) complete (C) create (D) gentle (E) point out

24. **corroborate** (A) help (B) conspire (C) stutter (D) corporeal (E) confirm

25. **antagonism** (A) hostility (B) apathy (C) agreement (D) complaisance
(E) affinity

26. **synthesis** (A) fake material (B) unification (C) harmony (D) synergy (E) analysis

18

PRACTICE SET 1

ANSWER KEY

1. C
2. B
3. A
4. D
5. C
6. A
7. E
8. D
9. C
10. C
11. A
12. B
13. A
14. A
15. D
16. C
17. A
18. B
19. A
20. D
21. B
22. D
23. C
24. E
25. A
26. B

DISPERSE   to spread out (v)

Synonyms:

Antonyms:

Context: The police ordered the crowd to **disperse** during the demonstration.

Self-Referential:

ECCENTRIC   unusual, strange (adj)

Synonyms:

Antonyms:

Context: It is a double standard that when rich people behave strangely, they are called **eccentric**, but when poor people are odd, they are just crazy.

Self-Referential:

REDUNDANT   repetitive, and thus unnecessary (adj)

Synonyms:

Antonyms:

Context: When my grandfather appeared wearing both suspenders and a belt to hold up his pants, my mom suggested that his accessories were a bit redundant.

Self-Referential:

PRECURSOR   a necessary predecessor (n)

Synonyms:

Antonyms:

Context: African-American blues is a **precursor** to contemporary rock-n-roll.

Self-Referential:

DEFER   to postpone, **or** to submit to another (v)

Synonyms:

Antonyms:

Context: Jane could **defer** her student loan payments for two years after joining the Peace Corps.

Jonathan decided to defer to his father when making financial judgments.

Self-Referential:

CATALYST   a thing that sets another in motion or causes change (n)

Synonyms:

Antonyms:

Context: The budget crisis was a **catalyst** for the city council to act on the bond issues.

Self-Referential:

DISARM   to deprive of weapons, **or** to win over, ingratiate(v)

Synonyms:

Antonyms:

Context: The SWAT team was able to **disarm** the sniper before he could hurt anyone.

I was disarmed by her sweet smile and generous nature.

Self-Referential:

PRONE   inclined, **or** the position of lying face down (adj)

Synonyms:

Antonyms:

Context: Matthew was **prone** to spend too much money while on dates.

I fell asleep while lying prone on the beach, and as a result got a terrible sunburn on my back and legs.

Self-Referential:

PROFOUND   deep, thoughtful (adj)

Synonyms:

Antonyms:

Context: The poetry of Wallace Stevens is extraordinarily **profound**, with evocative imagery and subtle language.

Self-Referential:

TORQUE   rotational force , twist (n)

Synonyms:

Antonyms:

Context: Because the lid of the jar was slippery, Greg could not apply enough **torque** to open it.

Self-Referential:

DIGRESS   to move away from (v)

Synonyms:

Antonyms:

Context: The professor continued to **digress** from the topic of discussion.

Self-Referential:

DIVERGE   to go apart in different directions (v)

Synonyms:

Antonyms:

Context: Although the sisters had been the closest of friends while growing up, their paths began to **diverge** when they became adults.

Self-Referential:

TANGENTIAL   peripheral, not on the subject at hand (adj)

Synonyms:

Antonyms:

Context: Spencer has only a **tangential** interest in metallurgy; his real interest is metallic sculpture.

Self-Referential:

POROUS   having pores, having minute holes (adj)

Synonyms:

Antonyms:

Context: Unfortunately, the lining of the landfill was extremely **porous**, and allowed waste to seep through.

Self-Referential:

PLUMMET   to fall suddenly (v)

Synonyms:

Antonyms:

Context: The skydiver **plummeted** toward the ground until her parachute opened.

Self-Referential:

CIRCUMLOCUTION   excessive speaking, wordiness (n)

Synonyms:

Antonyms:

Context: The candidate's **circumlocution** prevented him from being well-received by the impatient audience.

Self-Referential:

PERTURB   to disquiet, upset (v)

Synonyms:

Antonyms:

Context: You cannot **perturb** my grandmother, she has seen everything.

Self-Referential:

OPAQUE   not transparent, not letting light through (adj)

Synonyms:

Antonyms:

Context: Simon hung **opaque** blue curtains in order to make his room cool and dark.

Self-Referential:

IMPENETRABLE   unable to be penetrated, pierced (adj)

Synonyms:

Antonyms:

Context: The wall around the ancient city was **impenetrable**, forcing the invading army to lay siege to the city.

Self-Referential:

DESICCATE   to dry out, dehydrate (v)

Synonyms:

Antonyms:

Context: Out in the desert, things tend to **desiccate** rapidly, preserving the remains of ancient Native American sites for centuries.

Self-Referential:

PHENOMENON   an occurrence (n)

Synonyms:

Antonyms:

Context: The aurora borealis is an exciting and colorful **phenomenon**.

Self-Referential:

TACIT   unspoken yet understood (adj)

Synonyms:

Antonyms:

Context: The two brothers had a **tacit** agreement not to compete against one another for the same girl.

Self-Referential:

WHIMSY   caprice, a playful thing (n)

Synonyms:

Antonyms:

Context: Putting the colorful streamers in the tree branches was pure **whimsy**.

Self-Referential:

ABSTRACT   theoretical (adj), **or** to summarize (v), **or** a summary (n)

Synonyms:

Antonyms:

Context: Justice is an **abstract** idea.

The assistant had to **abstract** all the relevant articles, so that his boss could get the gist of them quickly.

The **abstract** at the beginning of the report indicated that it was not pertinent to Jenny's paper.

Self-Referential:

INHERENT   in the essential nature of a thing (adj)

Synonyms:

Antonyms:

Context: It is an **inherent** characteristic of dogs that they devotedly follow their master.

Self-Referential:

DUBIOUS   doubtful, questionable (adj)

Synonyms:

Antonyms:

Context: The painting, which looked like a Picasso, was of **dubious** authenticity.

Self-Referential:

PLATITUDE   a trite saying, bromide (n)

Synonyms:

Antonyms:

Context: Whenever Mike complained about having to walk to school, his father would start spouting the usual **platitudes** about when he was Mike's age.

Self-Referential:

PRACTICE SET 2

Instructions: Circle the answer that most closely approximates the definition of the word given.

1. **redundant**   (A) idiotic   (B) repetitive   (C) bouncing back   (D) smelly   (E) useful

2. **inherent**   (A) essential   (B) internal   (C) explicit   (D) artificial   (E) added on

3. **defer**   (A) modest   (B) give away   (C) explain   (D) postpone   (E) help

4. **disperse**   (A) pay a salary   (B) change color   (C) disgraced   (D) frankness
   (E) spread out

5. **phenomenon**   (A) philosophy   (B) circumstance   (C) occurrence   (D) surroundings
   (E) ambivalence

6. **platitude**   (A) simile   (B) psalm   (C) paean   (D) dull saying   (E) flatness

7. **prone**   (A) libel   (B) lying on one's back   (C) cornbread   (D) inclined
   (E) flattering

8. **plummet**   (A) fall   (B) small fruit   (C) sound depth   (D) feel indifferent
   (E) a tiny plume

9. **eccentric**   (A) wobbly   (B) unusual   (C) wealthy   (D) elderly   (E) flashy

10. **desiccate**   (A) examine internal organs   (B) destroy   (C) blow up
    (D) dehydrate   (E) desert

11. **digress**   (A) exit   (B) recapitulate   (C) move away from   (D) talk too much
    (E) varying

12. **dubious**   (A) artful   (B) fraudulent   (C) exposed   (D) slight   (E) questionable

13. **precursor**   (A) predecessor   (B) successor   (C) peer   (D) contemporaneous
    (E) unstable

14. **opaque**   (A) transparent   (B) filmy   (C) well-lit   (D) shiny
    (E) not letting light through

15. **profound**   (A) bountiful   (B) thoughtful   (C) forage   (D) done in advance
    (E) secular

16. **catalyst**   (A) waterfall   (B) stuporous   (C) agent of change   (D) exhaust filter
    (E) brigand

17. **porous**   (A) soft   (B) impervious   (C) having an odor   (D) having holes
    (E) having a smooth surface

18. **diverge**   (A) come together   (B) assimilate   (C) spread thin   (D) separate
    (E) sell one's holdings in

19. **disarm** (A) win over (B) disgust (C) anger (D) poise (E) mutilate

20. **perturb** (A) disquiet (B) serene (C) change (D) educate (E) settle

21. **torque** (A) orbital collision (B) rotational force (C) circular reasoning (D) spherical implosion (E) gravitational pull

22. **tacit** (A) small cup (B) expressed without words (C) explicitly stated (D) reticent (E) social grace

23. **tangential** (A) circular (B) drawn out (C) borrowed (D) pungent (E) peripheral

24. **abstract** (A) modern (B) concrete (C) philosophical (D) summarize (E) small part

25. **impenetrable** (A) thick (B) dark (C) unpierceable (D) unpredictable (E) false

26. **whimsy** (A) caprice (B) drunk (C) wordy (D) windmill (E) streamer

27. **circumlocution** (A) periphery (B) wordiness (C) angularity (D) prudence (E) caution

PRACTICE SET 2

ANSWER KEY

1. B
2. A
3. D
4. E
5. C
6. D
7. D
8. A
9. B
10. D
11. C
12. E
13. A
14. E
15. B
16. C
17. D
18. D
19. A
20. A
21. B
22. B
23. E
24. D
25. C
26. A
27. B

FALLACY   a logical flaw, mistake (n)

Synonyms:

Antonyms:

Context: The **fallacy** of Ralph's argument lay in his erroneous assumptions about nature.

Self-Referential:

DEMUR   to hesitate, protest (v)

Synonyms:

Antonyms:

Context: When offered lemon meringue pie, Jeremy felt he could not **demur**.

Self-Referential:

ASSERT   to state without need of proof (v)

Synonyms:

Antonyms:

Context: Wendy is going to **assert** her claim to her grandmother's legacy.

Self-Referential:

REFUTE   to disprove, to argue against (v)

Synonyms:

Antonyms:

Context: Barbara could not **refute** the argument in favor of the new tax structure.

Self-Referential:

INQUISITIVE   curious, seeking knowledge (adj)

Synonyms:

Antonyms:

Context: My kitten is very **inquisitive**; she gets into every basket and box in my room.

Self-Referential:

MUNDANE   everyday, pedestrian (adj)

Synonyms:

Antonyms:

Context: Harold did not want to be concerned with such **mundane** chores as grocery shopping and housecleaning.

Self-Referential:

COHERENT   intelligible, consistent (adj)

Synonyms:

Antonyms:

Context: Carolyn could not make a **coherent** statement after witnessing the disastrous flood.

Self-Referential:

EQUIVOCAL   wavering, vacillating (adj)

Synonyms:

Antonyms:

Context: The politician's **equivocal** reply to the reporter's question was seen by the opposition as flip-flopping.

Self-Referential:

HARANGUE   long, complaining speech (n)

Synonyms:

Antonyms:

Context: Peter's **harangue** concerning the hotel's lack of service was embarrassing to his companions.

Self-Referential:

JARGON specialized vocabulary (n)

Synonyms:

Antonyms:

Context: The scientist could not explain her research without using a lot of highly technical **jargon**.

Self-Referential:

SUCCINCT concise, stating in few words (adj)

Synonyms:

Antonyms:

Context: Bill could not state his opinion **succinctly**, he went on and on until most of the audience had left.

Self-Referential:

DIFFUSE to spread thinly (v), **or** scattered (adj)

Synonyms:

Antonyms:

Context: The firefighters tried to **diffuse** the noxious fumes by ventilating the area.

The **diffuse** particles of soot and ash fell all over town.

Self-Referential:

ARTICULATE well-spoken, intelligible (adj), **or** to speak clearly and distinctly (v)

Synonyms:

Antonyms:

Context: Our class valedictorian is an extremely **articulate** and poised young man.

The rock singer could **articulate** the jumbled emotions felt by the teenagers.

Self-Referential:

GARRULOUS   extremely talkative (adj)

Synonyms:

Antonyms:

Context: Hilary is a **garrulous** child; she just chatters constantly to anyone who will listen.

Self-Referential:

ORATE   to make a speech, esp. pompously (v)

Synonyms:

Antonyms:

Context: Carrie was prepared to **orate** at great length on the evils of strong drink.

Self-Referential:

LACONIC   of few words, reticent (adj)

Synonyms:

Antonyms:

Context: Calvin Coolidge was so famous for his **laconic** nature that he was nicknamed 'Silent Cal.'

Self-Referential:

OBSCURE   to hide (v), **or** hidden, vague, not easily understood (adj)

Synonyms:

Antonyms:

Context: The clouds **obscured** the sunlight.

          An **obscure** historical figure was the basis for Joan's next book.

Self-Referential:

CHICANERY   flim-flam, trickery (n)

Synonyms:

Antonyms:

Context: The salesman's **chicanery** led to Terry's purchase of many items she did not need.

Self-Referential:

FURTIVE   secret, sneaky (adj)

Synonyms:

Antonyms:

Context: The weasel seemed **furtive** as it scurried through the underbrush with its prey in its mouth.

Self-Referential:

VOLATILE   unstable, likely to explode or vaporize (adj)

Synonyms:

Antonyms:

Context: The oils used in preparing the perfume are highly **volatile** and must be kept tightly sealed.

Self-Referential:

EXTEMPORIZE   to speak spontaneously (v)

Synonyms:

Antonyms:

Context: Diane is so smart that she is able to **extemporize** on virtually any subject.

Self-Referential:

ZEALOT   one who has great enthusiasm, esp. for a cause (n)

Synonyms:

Antonyms:

Context: When it comes to voting rights, Nelson has always been a **zealot**.

Self-Referential:

ESPOUSE   to take to oneself, to adopt a belief (v)

Synonyms:

Antonyms:

Context: Ronnie **espoused** the most peculiar beliefs about the economy.

Self-Referential:

PROVOCATIVE   tending to stimulate (adj)

Synonyms:

Antonyms:

Context: Ben's proposal for changing the system of management was **provocative**; the whole office debated its merits.

Self-Referential:

SUPERFLUOUS   excess, extra (adj)

Synonyms:

Antonyms:

Context: After the party, the **superfluous** refreshments were taken to the children.

Self-Referential:

EXPEND   to use up (v)

Synonyms:

Antonyms:

Context: Margaret could not **expend** too much energy keeping up with her six
                 grandchildren, or she would collapse from exhaustion.

Self-Referential:

PRACTICE SET 3

Instructions: Circle the answer that most closely approximates the definition of the word given.

1. **jargon**   (A) unnerving thing   (B) small boat   (C) wisdom   (D) special vocabulary   (E) slang

2. **assert**   (A) property   (B) opine   (C) positive quality   (D) adjust   (E) state as fact

3. **obscure**   (A) transparent   (B) conceal   (C) lighten   (D) interpret   (E) tiny

4. **provocative**   (A) belligerent   (B) approximate   (C) stimulating   (D) judicious   (E) prolonged

5. **fallacy**   (A) error   (B) believability   (C) stammering   (D) fancy ornament   (E) good idea

6. **volatile**   (A) nimble   (B) willful   (C) unstable   (D) permanent   (E) incessant

7. **articulate**   (A) inchoate   (B) babble   (C) speak clearly   (D) talented   (E) solid

8. **expend**   (A) use up   (B) conserve   (C) mete out   (D) ration   (E) give away

9. **inquisitive**   (A) complacent   (B) curious   (C) terrifying   (D) querulous   (E) resolvable

10. **chicanery**   (A) fashionableness   (B) affectation   (C) skillfulness   (D) quarrelsomeness   (E) trickery

11. **orate**   (A) pray   (B) think deeply   (C) speak   (D) experiment   (E) sing loudly

12. **refute**   (A) admit   (B) argue against   (C) justify   (D) discard   (E) fugitive

13. **zealot**   (A) crank   (B) eccentric   (C) apathetic person   (D) enthusiast   (E) orthodox

14. **equivocal**   (A) identical   (B) in unison   (C) unambiguous   (D) uncertain   (E) truthful

15. **furtive**   (A) overt   (B) passionate   (C) stealthy   (D) violent   (E) excited

16. **demur**   (A) object   (B) modest   (C) denude   (D) incorruptible   (E) solemn

17. **succinct**   (A) sharp   (B) juicy   (C) concise   (D) submit   (E) abrupt

18. **extemporize**   (A) wait   (B) make anachronistic   (C) arrange   (D) speak spontaneously   (E) justify

19. **superfluous**   (A) contemptuous   (B) excessive   (C) insignificant   (D) most superior   (E) essential

20. **mundane**   (A) everyday   (B) sacred   (C) poetic   (D) interesting   (E) onerous

21. **laconic** (A) laid back (B) lazy (C) prompt (D) anxious (E) terse

22. **espouse** (A) adopt (B) divorce (C) discover (D) escape (E) shield

23. **coherent** (A) incomprehensible (B) fellow believer (C) at the same time
(D) intelligible (E) chaotic

24. **diffuse** (A) propitiate (B) reconcile (C) spread thin (D) unlike (E) tranquilize

25. **harangue** (A) shrew (B) inspirational sermon (C) complaining speech (D)
presage (E) regret

26. **garrulous** (A) belligerent (B) talkative (C) hirsute (D) gaudy
(E) simple-minded

PRACTICE SET 3

ANSWER KEY

1. D
2. E
3. B
4. C
5. A
6. C
7. C
8. A
9. B
10. E
11. C
12. B
13. D
14. D
15. C
16. A
17. C
18. D
19. B
20. A
21. E
22. A
23. D
24. C
25. C
26. B

MALEVOLENT   evil, having evil intent (adj)

Synonyms:

Antonyms:

Context: The dragon had a **malevolent** gleam in its eye as it pounced upon the unwary travelers.

Self-Referential:

PARAGON   an ideal, a perfect model (n)

Synonyms:

Antonyms:

Context: With his great physique and good looks, Howard was a **paragon** of virility.

Self-Referential:

NULLIFY   negate, make invalid (v)

Synonyms:

Antonyms:

Context: The hockey team captain's cheating led the commissioner to **nullify** the team's winning score.

Self-Referential:

CONSUMMATE   complete, accomplish (v); **or** perfect, to a high degree (adj)

Synonyms:

Antonyms:

Context: The lawyers **consummated** the settlement over a champagne toast.

It was a **consummate** performance of the piano concerto, with both artistic and technical perfection achieved.

Self-Referential:

ARDUOUS   difficult, strenuous (adj)

Synonyms:

Antonyms:

Context: It was an especially **arduous** climb; all the mountaineers were exhausted when it was over.

Self-Referential:

FELICITY   happiness, pleasantness (n)

Synonyms:

Antonyms:

Context: We might live in even more **felicity** if we were married.

Self-Referential:

PRODIGY   very talented child (n)

Synonyms:

Antonyms:

Context: The Harrisons suspected their daughter was a **prodigy** when she was doing multiplication at the age of three.

Self-Referential:

GUILE   cunning, trickery (n)

Synonyms:

Antonyms:

Context: Herman used **guile** to insinuate himself into the exclusive party.

Self-Referential:

INGENIOUS   extremely clever, original (adj)

Synonyms:

Antonyms:

Context: At its first appearance in 1879, the telephone was seen as an **ingenious** device.

Self-Referential:

IMPERATIVE   necessary, immediately important (adj)

Synonyms:

Antonyms:

Context: It was **imperative** that the messenger see the general before the battle commenced.

Self-Referential:

CONSTRAIN   restrict, confine (v)

Synonyms:

Antonyms:

Context: It was impossible to **constrain** the children within the bounds of behavior acceptable in a china shop.

Self-Referential:

SUPPRESS   keep secret, contain, inhibit (v)

Synonyms:

Antonyms:

Context: Information about the CIA's covert operations in the former Soviet Union has been **suppressed** for decades.

Self-Referential:

CAPITULATE   give in, surrender (v)

Synonyms:

Antonyms:

Context: The Confederate Army was more than ready to **capitulate** when Lee finally surrendered at the Appomattox Courthouse.

Self-Referential:

OBSEQUIOUS sycophantic, fawning (adj)

Synonyms:

Antonyms:

Context: Groupies are an **obsequious** sort; they are constantly ingratiating themselves with their idol, or some member of their idol's entourage.

Self-Referential:

PLACATE please, pacify (v)

Synonyms:

Antonyms:

Context: A six-year-old having a tantrum cannot be **placated**; he will fuss long after you give him what he wants.

Self-Referential:

AFFLUENT wealthy (adj)

Synonyms:

Antonyms:

Context: Adrienne was from a very **affluent** family, she never lacked for anything.

Self-Referential:

ZEAL fanatical enthusiasm (n)

Synonyms:

Antonyms:

Context: The **zeal** of the candidate's followers was so great as to be frightening at times.

Self-Referential:

INHIBIT   restrain, forbid (v)

Synonyms:

Antonyms:

Context: No American can be **inhibited** from practicing her or his religion, no matter how peculiar.

Self-Referential:

PLASTICITY   malleability, stretchiness (adj)

Synonyms:

Antonyms:

Context: The modeling clay needed more water added to it in order to regain its **plasticity**.

Self-Referential:

CYNIC   one who has an attitude of contempt, distrust (n)

Synonyms:

Antonyms:

Context: Those who break the law solely because others do so are the worst kind of **cynic**.

Self-Referential:

BOLSTER   support (v)

Synonyms:

Antonyms:

Context: Henry attempted to **bolster** his argument with irrelevant considerations and unfounded assumptions.

Self-Referential:

RESOLUTE   determined, faithful (adj)

Synonyms:

Antonyms:

Context: Kate was **resolute** in her decision to marry Keith.

Self-Referential:

CONNOISSEUR   one who appreciates fine things (n)

Synonyms:

Antonyms:

Context: Grace was a **connoisseur** of haute cuisine as well as nouvelle cuisine.

Self-Referential:

DECOROUS   in good taste, very proper (adj)

Synonyms:

Antonyms:

Context: At the garden party, the children were expected to behave in an appropriately **decorous** manner.

Self-Referential:

EUPHEMISM   mild word or phrase substituted for an offensive one (n)

Synonyms:

Antonyms:

Context: The politician's speech was full of **euphemisms** and buzzwords; he never said exactly what he meant.

Self-Referential:

PEDANTIC   overly scholarly (adj)

Synonyms:

Antonyms:

Context: Carroll was being **pedantic** by insisting on double checking every fact in the story.

Self-Referential:

BOMBAST   pompous speech (n)

Synonyms:

Antonyms:

Context: Although he said a few things of substance, the congressman's speech was mostly **bombast**.

Self-Referential:

PRACTICE SET 4

Instructions: Circle the answer that most closely approximates the definition of the word given.

1. **nullify** (A) appeal (B) obey (C) mix up (D) gather together (E) negate

2. **inhibit** (A) expose (B) restrain (C) relax (D) display (E) reside

3. **felicity** (A) cattiness (B) wildness (C) happiness (D) sentience (E) femininity

4. **connoisseur** (A) snob (B) implication (C) conspirator (D) one with refined tastes (E) one who knows wines

5. **capitulate** (A) repeat (B) take advantage of (C) surrender (D) legislate (E) defeat

6. **ingenious** (A) clever (B) candid (C) gullible (D) overt (E) disreputable

7. **malevolent** (A) smelly (B) draconian (C) excessively ugly (D) clumsy (E) evil

8. **bombast** (A) explosiveness (B) humility (C) ambush (D) artillery (E) pompous speech

9. **constrain** (A) release (B) confine (C) immodesty (D) interpret (E) endure

10. **euphemism** (A) sermon (B) harmony (C) simple word in place of complex (D) curse word (E) mild word in place of offensive

11. **consummate** (A) clear soup (B) unfinished (C) perfect (D) used up (E) tubercular

12. **resolute** (A) hindered (B) determined (C) judgmental (D) timid (E) equivocal

13. **placate** (A) flatten (B) disturb (C) calm (D) locate precisely (E) braid

14. **bolster** (A) ball-shaped (B) braggart (C) erupt (D) support (E) excite

15. **paragon** (A) contradiction (B) theoretical framework (C) ideal (D) jumble (E) two-sided figure

16. **pedantic** (A) hanging down (B) ignorant (C) nonconformist (D) servile (E) overly scholarly

17. **guile** (A) cunning (B) innocence (C) direction (D) pretext (E) thin coat

18. **arduous** (A) artistic (B) difficult (C) artistic (D) silvery (E) stubborn

19. **cynic** (A) doubter (B) evil person (C) sarcastic person (D) contemptuous person (E) snide person

20. **imperative** (A) authoritative (B) arrogant (C) urgently needed (D) endangered (E) reckless

21. **decorous** (A) ornamental (B) phony (C) decaying (D) proper (E) dilapidated

22. **prodigy** (A) offspring (B) talented child (C) honesty (D) wasteful person (E) goading person

23. **zeal** (A) humor (B) apex (C) pungency (D) supremacy (E) enthusiasm

24. **suppress** (A) keep secret (B) put under water (C) assume (D) exploit (E) excel

25. **obsequious** (A) deferential (B) stubborn (C) ungovernable (D) offensive (E) unmindful

26. **plasticity** (A) aphoristicness (B) phoniness (C) malleability (D) horizontalness (E) believability

27. **affluent** (A) impoverished (B) influential (C) avaricious (D) ruthless (E) wealthy

PRACTICE SET 4
ANSWER KEY

1. E
2. B
3. C
4. D
5. C
6. A
7. E
8. E
9. B
10. E
11. C
12. B
13. C
14. D
15. C
16. E
17. A
18. B
19. D
20. C
21. D
22. B
23. E
24. A
25. A
26. C
27. E

ARROGANT	overbearing, proud (adj)
Synonyms:	
Antonyms:	
Context:	George was awfully **arrogant,** strutting around as though he owned the place.
Self-Referential:	

MISANTHROPE	one who hates humanity (n)
Synonyms:	
Antonyms:	
Context:	Lex was so angry at the whole world for so long that he became a **misanthrope**.
Self-Referential:	

JEER to taunt, deride (v)

Synonyms:

Antonyms:

Context: The crowd **jeered** at the pitcher after he walked three batters.

Self-Referential:

DISINGENUOUS seemingly honest while not being so (adj)

Synonyms:

Antonyms:

Context: Clyde was **disingenuous** with his date when he asked her if she wanted to see his etchings.

Self-Referential:

PROPRIETY appropriateness, social acceptability (n)

Synonyms:

Antonyms:

Context: The **propriety** of Miss Manners' behavior is above question.

Self-Referential:

HERETIC one who holds unorthodox or unapproved beliefs (n)

Synonyms:

Antonyms:

Context: Jones was considered a **heretic** by other economists for his radical views of economic growth.

Self-Referential:

AUTHENTIC genuine, trustworthy (adj)

Synonyms:

Antonyms:

Context: The feelings expressed by the suitors were undoubtedly **authentic**

Self-Referential:

ERADICATE   to eliminate completely (v)

Synonyms:

Antonyms:

Context: Cheryl could not **eradicate** the cockroaches from her apartment, so she called a professional exterminator.

Self-Referential:

GIST   general meaning, essence (n)

Synonyms:

Antonyms:

Context: Although he was not fluent in French, Gus could catch the **gist** of the French song's lyrics.

Self-Referential:

OBJECTIVE   empirically provable, existing independently (adj)

Synonyms:

Antonyms:

Context: The three witnesses told the same story, so the detective knew that the incident was an **objective** fact.

Self-Referential:

AFFILIATION   connection, association (n)

Synonyms:

Antonyms:

Context: Jeanne went to Notre Dame High School, which has no **affiliation** with the famous college of the same name.

Self-Referential:

APPOSITE   relevant, to the point (adj)

Synonyms:

Antonyms:

Context: Gretchen's comments were **apposite** to the discussion, and clarified many points.

Self-Referential:

ANTITHESIS   direct opposite (n)

Synonyms:

Antonyms:

Context: Gail's ideas were the **antithesis** of good taste and discretion; her notions were downright vulgar.

Self-Referential:

HETEROGENEOUS mixed, made up of unlike elements (adj)

Synonyms:

Antonyms:

Context: Sam's store offers a **heterogeneous** assortment of goods, from hardware to lingerie.

Self-Referential:

STEREOTYPE   a generalized judgment of a group (n)

Synonyms:

Antonyms:

Context: Sally does not fit the **stereotype** of the airheaded sorority girl; she is a dedicated student and a committed volunteer.

Self-Referential:

PARADIGM   model, theoretical framework (n)

Synonyms:

Antonyms:

Context: The architectural drawings combined design elements to form a **paradigm** of an energy efficient work space.

Self-Referential:

PRECEDENT   earlier example setting a rule (n)

Synonyms:

Antonyms:

Context: The issues in the computer piracy case were so new that the judge had no **precedent** on which to base her decision.

Self-Referential:

CONFORM   to adapt or be compliant with (v)

Synonyms:

Antonyms:

Context: Rachel was not ready to **conform** to the expectations of others; she was essentially a free spirit.

Self-Referential:

CORRESPOND   to match, to conform, to parallel (v)

Synonyms:

Antonyms:

Context: The fraudulent painting **corresponded** in every way to the original but one: the paint on the forgery was still wet.

Self-Referential:

DISSENT   to disagree (v)

Synonyms:

Antonyms:

Context: Because he does not share the opinions of the newer justices, Justice Stevens frequently **dissents** on most issues.

Self-Referential:

NUANCE   slight distinction, shade of difference (n)

Synonyms:

Antonyms:

Context: Although the young performer played every note of the concerto correctly, he failed to express fully every **nuance** of emotion implicit in the piece.

Self-Referential:

NEGLIGIBLE   insignificant, not to be considered (adj)

Synonyms:

Antonyms:

Context: The effect that one more grain of sand, more or less, had on the entire beach was **negligible**.

Self-Referential:

TRIVIAL   minor, not important (adj)

Synonyms:

Antonyms:

Context: The judge decided her complaints were **trivial**, and awarded her no compensation.

Self-Referential:

SUBORDINATE   depending on, subservient to (adj)

Synonyms:

Antonyms:

Context: Melanie was uncomfortable in the role of a **subordinate** housewife, so she decided to get a divorce.

Self-Referential:

DEPLETION   lessening (n)

Synonyms:

Antonyms:

Context: The **depletion** of the water supply was of grave concern to the town council, because they were faced with a major drought.

Self-Referential:

ALLOY   a mixture, esp. of metal (n)

Synonyms:

Antonyms:

Context: The sword was made of a strange **alloy** that would not break.

Self-Referential:

ECLECTIC   having varying elements (adj)

Synonyms:

Antonyms:

Context: Jane's house was decorated with an **eclectic** blend of Victoriana and Southwest Mission style.

Self-Referential:

PRACTICE SET 5

Instructions: Circle the answer that most closely approximates the definition of the word given.

1. **authentic** (A) self-taught (B) real (C) orthodox (D) expert (E) scientific

2. **conform** (A) abridge (B) disagree (C) complex (D) establish (E) adapt

3. **arrogant** (A) haughty (B) take command (C) pointed (D) humble
(E) supplicant

4. **disingenuous** (A) honest (B) insincere (C) decomposing (D) apathetic
(E) extricated

5. **gist** (A) talent (B) teasing (C) resources (D) essence (E) cartilage

6. **affiliation** (A) tenderness (B) dislike (C) ratification (D) association
(E) pretentiousness

7. **trivial** (A) three-legged (B) quiet (C) minor (D) overheated (E) important

8. **heterogeneous** (A) mixed (B) of similar parts (C) straight (D) unorthodox
(E) of different species

9. **eradicate** (A) unambiguous (B) profligate (C) propagate (D) equivocate
(E) eliminate

10. **negligible** (A) noteworthy (B) insignificant (C) indifferent (D) careless
(E) pessimist

11. **antithesis** (A) juxtaposition (B) hatred (C) opposite (D) treatise (E) expectant

12. **misanthrope** (A) recluse (B) woman-hater (C) philosopher (D) people-hater
(E) barbarian

13. **heretic** (A) brave (B) experimenter (C) ascetic person (D) sealed
(E) unorthodox person

14. **paradigm** (A) point in time (B) theoretical framework (C) seeming contradiction
(D) ideal (E) extremely important

15. **jeer** (A) applaud (B) banter (C) taunt (D) pry (E) trifle

16. **objective** (A) visualized (B) independently true (C) offensive (D) compliant
(E) protesting

17. **stereotype** (A) species (B) type size (C) sound system (D) generalization
(E) racist remark

18. **nuance** (A) indiscriminate (B) small distance (C) distraction (D) eccentricity
(E) slight difference

19. **correspond**   (A) agree (B) indoctrinate (C) groove (D) manage (E) return

20. **subordinate**   (A) rebellious (B) abet (C) induce to perjure (D) subservient (E) latent

21. **apposite**   (A) facade (B) relevant (C) assigned (D) not alike (E) unessential

22. **precedent**   (A) imploring (B) superiority (C) example (D) cliff (E) exact

23. **dissent**   (A) support (B) upset (C) disagree (D) separate (E) unify

24. **depletion**   (A) cheapening (B) turpitude (C) finishing (D) reduction (E) production

25. **eclectic**   (A) concealing (B) having seizures (C) brilliant (D) powerful (E) mixed

26. **propriety**   (A) atonement (B) appropriateness (C) indecency (D) auspiciousness (E) relativeness

27. **alloy**   (A) mixture (B) friend (C) relieve (D) small road (E) permit

PRACTICE SET 5
ANSWER KEY

1. B
2. E
3. A
4. B
5. D
6. D
7. C
8. A
9. E
10. B
11. C
12. D
13. E
14. B
15. C
16. B
17. D
18. E
19. A
20. D
21. B
22. C
23. C
24. D
25. E
26. B
27. A

CONVOLUTED   intricate, coiled, twisted (adj)

Synonyms:

Antonyms:

Context: Samantha's explanation of her actions was a **convoluted** series of lies and misapprehensions.

Self-Referential:

INEXTRICABLE   not able to be untangled (adj)

Synonyms:

Antonyms:

Context: Marla found herself in **inextricable** difficulties, of which she could see no end.

Self-Referential:

LABYRINTH   maze (n)

Synonyms:

Antonyms:

Context: The topiary **labyrinth** was too difficult for Allison; she could not find her way out.

Self-Referential:

MULTIFARIOUS   diverse, of great variety (adj)

Synonyms:

Antonyms:

Context: Jeremy's knowledge of history and society was both **multifarious** and recondite.

Self-Referential:

CONSOLIDATE   to join together, merge (v)

Synonyms:

Antonyms:

Context: Kenneth decided to **consolidate** his financial obligations into one bank loan.

Self-Referential:

COMPONENT   essential element, part (n)

Synonyms:

Antonyms:

Context: The musical score was only one **component** leading to the success
                of the show.

Self-Referential:

SHARD   fragment, esp. of glass or pottery (n)

Synonyms:

Antonyms:

Context: Dr. Leakey found a pottery **shard** dating back at least 10,000 years.

Self-Referential:

COMPREHENSIVE all-inclusive (adj)

Synonyms:

Antonyms:

Context: The new law was **comprehensive** in its prohibition of pollution.

Self-Referential:

PERVASIVE   throughout, in every part (adj)

Synonyms:

Antonyms:

Context: The sappy music was so **pervasive** you could hear it in every room
                of the house.

Self-Referential:

PLETHORA   multiplicity, excessive amount (n)

Synonyms:

Antonyms:

Context: Arthur had a **plethora** of armaments in his extensive collection.

Self-Referential:

FRACAS   riot, fight (n)

Synonyms:

Antonyms:

Context: Leonard was drawn into the **fracas** against his better judgment.

Self-Referential:

GRATUITOUS   uncalled for, not warranted (adj)

Synonyms:

Antonyms:

Context: Shopping with Beth was an exercise in **gratuitous** spending; she bought everything in sight.

Self-Referential:

PANDEMONIUM   noisy chaos, bedlam (n)

Synonyms:

Antonyms:

Context: The birthday party dissolved into **pandemonium** when the piñata was smashed open.

Self-Referential:

SPORADIC   occasional, infrequent (adj)

Synonyms:

Antonyms:

Context: After the hurricane passed, **sporadic** rainfall continued for several days.

Self-Referential:

PROLOGUE   introductory passage (n)

Synonyms:

Antonyms:

Context: In the **prologue** to her book, Esther acknowledged her mentor's influence.

Self-Referential:

INCIPIENT   beginning, budding (adj)

Synonyms:

Antonyms:

Context: Although she had taken only three lessons, Becky felt herself to be an **incipient** violinist.

Self-Referential:

DEFINITIVE   authoritative (adj)

Synonyms:

Antonyms:

Context: Dan felt that he had written the **definitive** biography of George Washington.

Self-Referential:

NEXUS   connection, center (n)

Synonyms:

Antonyms:

Context: The new freeway is intended to be a **nexus** of the east and west parts of town.

Self-Referential:

SEQUENTIAL   in order, arranged serially (adj)

Synonyms:

Antonyms:

Context: The magazines were not **sequential**, so John had to look through all of them in order to find the article he wanted.

Self-Referential:

CONFLATE   to blend together, esp. a text (v)

Synonyms:

Antonyms:

Context: Many scholars believe this classical epic is **conflated**, having been written in two distinct periods of ancient history.

Self-Referential:

QUORUM   number of members of a governing body necessary in order to proceed (n)

Synonyms:

Antonyms:

Context: Not having a **quorum** present, the city council was unable to make a decision regarding the new ordinance.

Self-Referential:

TROUPE group of performers (n)

Synonyms:

Antonyms:

Context: The **troupe** of dancers was ready and eager to perform that night.

Self-Referential:

INTRINSIC of the essential nature of a thing (adj)

Synonyms:

Antonyms:

Context: In his series of investigative articles, Theodore was able to uncover the **intrinsic** corruption of the whole organization.

Self-Referential:

ORTHODOX adhering to a strict set of beliefs (adj)

Synonyms:

Antonyms:

Context: The family belonged to an **orthodox** sect of Mormons that still practiced polygamy.

Self-Referential:

MAVERICK intrepid person, innovator (n)

Synonyms:

Antonyms:

Context: In his time, Zack was considered a **maverick**, although now his ideas seem commonplace.

Self-Referential:

ABERRANT deviating from the norm (adj)

Synonyms:

Antonyms:

Context: People see in his works a diseased and **aberrant** genius.

Self-Referential:

PRACTICE SET 6

Instructions: Circle the answer that most closely approximates the definition of the word given.

1. **fracas**   (A) crack   (B) blemish   (C) riot   (D) sliver   (E) stew

2. **inextricable**   (A) impossible   (B) knitted   (C) inevitable   (D) difficult   (E) tangled

3. **quorum**   (A) number of people voting   (B) meeting place
   (C) number of people in a line   (D) number of people needed at a meeting   (E) former

4. **multifarious**   (A) containing iron   (B) diverse   (C) evil   (D) angular
   E) many-sided

5. **plethora**   (A) excessive amount   (B) majority   (C) shortage   (D) pedestal
   (E) paucity

6. **consolidate**   (A) compose   (B) comfort   (C) thicken   (D) merge   (E) associate

7. **convoluted**   (A) frenzied   (B) festive   (C) twisted   (D) simple   (E) spastic

8. **orthodox**   (A) having liberal beliefs   (B) beginning   (C) agnostic
   (D) having straight teeth   (E) conformist

9. **shard**   (A) predator   (B) fragment   (C) totality   (D) bitter   (E) fake

10. **labyrinth**   (A) tear-like   (B) lip-like   (C) research facility   (D) maze
    (E) industrious

11. **incipient**   (A) mediocre   (B) beginning   (C) final   (D) hinting   (E) musical

12. **maverick**   (A) nonconformist   (B) disciplinarian   (C) wealthy person
    (D) knowledgeable person   (E) singer

13. **pandemonium**   (A) wide view   (B) harmony   (C) equipment   (D) confusion
    (E) fellowship

14. **component**   (A) environment   (B) element   (C) composer   (D) simultaneous
    (E) agreement

15. **definitive**   (A) faulty   (B) circumspect   (C) authoritative   (D) incomplete
    (E) unintelligible

16. **aberrant**   (A) accomplice   (B) concise   (C) consumed   (D) penitent   (E) deviant

17. **pervasive**   (A) agitated   (B) loud   (C) superficial   (D) throughout   (E) distorted

18. **comprehensive**   (A) densified   (B) all-inclusive   (C) understandable   (D) piecemeal
    (E) narrow

19. **prologue** (A) denouement (B) introductory passage (C) afterward (D) lengthen (E) path

20. **gratuitous** (A) thankful (B) unwarranted (C) silly (D) contented (E) graceful

21. **conflate** (A) blend (B) edit (C) force air out (D) write (E) fill with air

22. **nexus** (A) axis (B) partition (C) subsequent (D) thorn (E) connection

23. **intrinsic** (A) complex (B) external (C) inherent (D) uncharacteristic (E) scheming

24. **sequential** (A) separate (B) mawkish (C) consecutive (D) recused (E) exclusive

25. **troupe** (A) defeat (B) trench (C) group of soldiers (D) absentee (E) group of performers

26. **sporadic** (A) unplanned (B) occasional (C) having seeds (D) parody-like (E) clumsy

68

PRACTICE SET 6
ANSWER KEY

1. C
2. E
3. D
4. B
5. A
6. D
7. C
8. E
9. B
10. D
11. B
12. A
13. D
14. B
15. C
16. E
17. D
18. B
19. B
20. B
21. A
22. E
23. C
24. C
25. E
26. B

ENUMERATE   to count (v)

Synonyms:

Antonyms:

Context: The purpose of a census is to **enumerate** all the residents of a country.

Self-Referential:

FUSION merging of diverse parts into a whole (n)

Synonyms:

Antonyms:

Context: The **fusion** of African and Caribbean musical styles with traditional French music created the unique zydeco style in Louisiana.

Self-Referential:

DICHOTOMY separation into two parts (n)

Synonyms:

Antonyms:

Context: In some schools of ancient Greek philosophy, there was a **dichotomy** between body and spirit.

Self-Referential:

ANACHRONISM a thing or person out of place in time (n)

Synonyms:

Antonyms:

Context: With his powdered wig and cutaway coat, Christopher was definitely an **anachronism**.

Self-Referential:

FLEDGLING young, inexperienced (adj)

Synonyms:

Antonyms:

Context: The **fledgling** architect had very little business at first, but after her first few projects, clients started to call her more.

Self-Referential:

EXIGENT   needing swift action (adj)

Synonyms:

Antonyms:

Context: There were more **exigent** demands placed on Harriet's time than raising begonias.

Self-Referential:

INOPPORTUNE   not timely, inappropriate (adj)

Synonyms:

Antonyms:

Context: The door-to-door salesman could not have arrived at Marcia's house at a more **inopportune** moment than when she was in the shower.

Self-Referential:

ALACRITY   promptness, eagerness (n)

Synonyms:

Antonyms:

Context: Xavier left a generous tip for the waiter who had served us with a refreshing **alacrity**.

Self-Referential:

ADJOURN   to suspend, as a meeting (v)

Synonyms:

Antonyms:

Context: The board decided to **adjourn** until the following week.

Self-Referential:

PREVALENT   common, frequent (adj)

Synonyms:

Antonyms:

Context: The use of that particular drug was not as **prevalent** as Judy's doctor led her to believe.

Self-Referential:

STASIS   stagnation, equilibrium (n)

Synonyms:

Antonyms:

Context: Without research and interaction between institutions, the academic community would find itself in a condition of **stasis**.

Self-Referential:

LABILE   unstable, open to change (adj)

Synonyms:

Antonyms:

Context: Andre's hypertension was considered **labile**; he was extremely susceptible to a heart attack.

Self-Referential:

EQUILIBRIUM   state of balance (n)

Synonyms:

Antonyms:

Context: The juggler held the bowling pin on his nose with perfect **equilibrium**.

Self-Referential:

RIVETING   commanding full attention, fascinating (adj)

Synonyms:

Antonyms:

Context: The audience found the demonstration of Native American war songs **riveting**.

Self-Referential:

CESSATION   stoppage, ceasing (n)

Synonyms:

Antonyms:

Context: The treaty called for a full **cessation** of all acts of war between the two countries.

Self-Referential:

RELINQUISH   to let go of, give up (v)

Synonyms:

Antonyms:

Context: Glenda could not bring herself to **relinquish** her son, even though she knew it would be better for him in the long run.

Self-Referential:

RENEGADE   an outlaw, one who is unconventional (n)

Synonyms:

Antonyms:

Context: Although he had committed no crime, Wesley was considered a **renegade** because he refused to cooperate with the authorities.

Self-Referential:

SUPERSEDE   to supplant (v)

Synonyms:

Antonyms:

Context: Typewriters have gradually been **superseded** by word processors and personal computers.

Self-Referential:

RECIPROCATE   to give and take, to return, to pay back (v)

Synonyms:

Antonyms:

Context: After being a guest at their dinner party, Rachel decided to **reciprocate** by having the Chesters over for cocktails.

Self-Referential:

CRUSADE   a zealous campaign for a cause (n)

Synonyms:

Antonyms:

Context: Lady Bird Johnson will be remembered for her **crusade** against litter and billboards.

Self-Referential:

SEMINAL   original, **or** relating to seeds or semen (adj)

Synonyms:

Antonyms:

Context: Her work was considered **seminal** in the field of anthropology.

The **seminal** fluid was frozen and preserved for later use.

Self-Referential:

ENDOW to grant, as a gift (v)

Synonyms:

Antonyms:

Context: Mr. Whitby decided to **endow** his alma mater by donating funds for a new library.

Self-Referential:

NUGATORY negligible, having no effect (adj)

Synonyms:

Antonyms:

Context: The additional expense of first class travel was **nugatory** for the corporate CEO.

Self-Referential:

UNASSAILABLE not questionable, not doubtable (adj)

Synonyms:

Antonyms:

Context: Mother Theresa's opinions regarding Christian charity are **unassailable**.

Self-Referential:

FLACCID limp, drooping (adj)

Synonyms:

Antonyms:

Context: The chef decided the noodles were overcooked because they were too **flaccid** for use in the lasagna.

Self-Referential:

DYNAMIC in motion (adj)

Synonyms:

Antonyms:

Context: The pianist gave a **dynamic** performance that was extraordinarily energetic.

Self-Referential:

PRACTICE SET 7

Instructions: Circle the answer that most closely approximates the definition of the word given.

1. **exigent** (A) sparse (B) depart (C) urgent (D) out of hand (E) acquitted

2. **enumerate** (A) count (B) speak clearly (C) mathematically inept (D) equivalent (E) connoisseur

3. **supersede** (A) conceal (B) come after (C) knock down (D) petition (E) supplant

4. **seminal** (A) half baked (B) original (C) studious (D) twice per year (E) linguistic

5. **alacrity** (A) fright (B) promptness (C) laziness (D) alarmist (E) arrangement

6. **dichotomy** (A) duality (B) leaf-bearer (C) colorful (D) lexicon (E) teaching

7. **reciprocate** (A) perform (B) formulate (C) interchange (D) narrate (E) reevaluate

8. **relinquish** (A) flavoring (B) survive (C) commit (D) give up (E) hesitate

9. **crusade** (A) horseback riding (B) shellfish (C) mixing pot (D) cause (E) voyage

10. **renegade** (A) outlaw (B) renewed (C) interpretation (D) counteractive (E) eminent

11. **endow** (A) bridal gift (B) give (C) completion (D) burden (E) persevere

12. **flaccid** (A) wet (B) limp (C) loose (D) linen (E) pendulous

13. **riveting** (A) severing (B) competing (C) fascinating (D) grandiose (E) formalizing

14. **adjourn** (A) associate (B) entreat (C) beside (D) indict (E) dismiss

15. **nugatory** (A) lumpy (B) pushy (C) annoying (D) eccentric (E) negligible

16. **dynamic** (A) static (B) explosive (C) familial (D) in motion (E) stubborn

17. **anachronism** (A) chronological error (B) metaphysical error (C) chronographical item (D) overdue (E) antedated thing

18. **cessation** (A) septic tank (B) ending (C) surety (D) incision (E) constriction

19. **inopportune** (A) ineffective (B) unusable (C) pardonable (D) untimely (E) dissenting

20. **unassailable** (A) indefensible (B) undoubtable (C) immodest (D) inaccessible (E) spurious

21. **fusion** (A) melding (B) splitting (C) bombast (D) hopelessness (E) gunfire

22. **prevalent** (A) rare (B) chic (C) reputable (D) apparent (E) frequent

23. **labile** (A) lip-like (B) toilsome (C) unstable (D) phonetic (E) tag-like

24. **fledgling** (A) winged (B) novice (C) experienced (D) pliant (E) woolen

25. **equilibrium** (A) balance (B) prevarication (C) asymmetry (D) vacillation (E) elegance

26. **stasis** (A) motion (B) condition (C) mastery (D) indolence (E) stagnation

PRACTICE SET 7
ANSWER KEY

1. C
2. A
3. E
4. B
5. B
6. A
7. C
8. D
9. D
10. A
11. B
12. B
13. C
14. E
15. E
16. D
17. A
18. B
19. D
20. B
21. A
22. E
23. C
24. B
25. A
26. E

VIABLE   capable of living, capable of working (adj)

Synonyms:

Antonyms:

Context: According to the engineers, the new photocopying method was simply not **viable**.

Self-Referential:

PROLIFERATE   to multiply, procreate (v)

Synonyms:

Antonyms:

Context: The ability of rabbits to **proliferate** rapidly is legendary.

Self-Referential:

FALLOW   barren, not cultivated or sown (adj)

Synonyms:

Antonyms:

Context: The cotton fields had to lie **fallow** every few years in order for the nutrients in the soil to replenish themselves.

Self-Referential:

FABRICATE   to create (v)

Synonyms:

Antonyms:

Context: She attempted to **fabricate** a story about her past life.

Self-Referential:

INCUBATION   period of gestation (n)

Synonyms:

Antonyms:

Context: The virus had a lengthy **incubation** period, ranging anywhere from thirty days to six months.

Self-Referential:

SUSCEPTIBLE   prone to, open to (adj)

Synonyms:

Antonyms:

Context: Ned was **susceptible** to respiratory infections, so he moved to Arizona.

Self-Referential:

PROPENSITY   inclination (n)

Synonyms:

Antonyms:

Context: Cheryl had a **propensity** for lying about her accomplishments.

Self-Referential:

COLLABORATE   to work together, to cooperate (v)

Synonyms:

Antonyms:

Context: The musicians decided to **collaborate** on the arrangement of the music.

Self-Referential:

CONNIVE   to conspire, to be in secret sympathy with (v)

Synonyms:

Antonyms:

Context: The historians have discovered that some of the villagers actually **connived** with the Nazis, while seeming to be neutral.

Self-Referential:

SYNCHRONOUS   at the same time (adj)

Synonyms:

Antonyms:

Context: The two dancers' leaps and twirls were precisely **synchronous** with one another.

Self-Referential:

RECALCITRANT   stubborn, defiant (adj)

Synonyms:

Antonyms:

Context: The **recalcitrant** teenager would not come out of his room except for meals and school.

Self-Referential:

BUCOLIC   pastoral, relating to country life (adj)

Synonyms:

Antonyms:

Context: Ginger wanted a **bucolic** cottage, with a white picket fence and a rose arbor.

Self-Referential:

UBIQUITOUS   everywhere, in all places (adj)

Synonyms:

Antonyms:

Context: If the tabloids are to be believed, Elvis is as **ubiquitous** as the air.

Self-Referential:

ACCULTURATE   to adapt to a culture (v)

Synonyms:

Antonyms:

Context: Caroline found it difficult to become **acculturated** to her new cnvironment.

Self-Referential:

COLOSSUS   giant statue, a very large thing (n)

Synonyms:

Antonyms:

Context: Few people know that the title of Emma Lazarus's famous poem on the Statue of Liberty is 'The New **Colossus**'.

Self-Referential:

DIMENSION   property of space, as in height, width, depth (n)

Synonyms:

Antonyms:

Context: Alex needed to know the **dimensions** of the painting in order to build a suitable frame.

Self-Referential:

BURGEON   to bloom, flourish (v)

Synonyms:

Antonyms:

Context: The traffic in African slaves was beginning to **burgeon** as early as the beginning of the 18th century.

Self-Referential:

CONTIGUOUS   adjacent to, with borders touching (adj)

Synonyms:

Antonyms:

Context: The Winthrops were proud of having visited all forty-eight **contiguous** states in the U.S.

Self-Referential:

RIFT　　　　　a gap or fissure (n)

Synonyms:

Antonyms:

Context:　　　　There was a **rift** the size of the Grand Canyon in their relationship.

Self-Referential:

RECAPITULATE　　to repeat, to sum up (v)

Synonyms:

Antonyms:

Context:　　　　The professor tried to **recapitulate** her entire lecture in the last five minutes of class.

Self-Referential:

TENUOUS　　　not solid, weak (adj)

Synonyms:

Antonyms:

Context:　　　　Mathilda had a very **tenuous** grasp of the concepts discussed in her philosophy class.

Self-Referential:

NADIR　　　low point, point opposite the zenith (n)

Synonyms:

Antonyms:

Context:　　　　The has-been actor felt he was at the **nadir** of his career when he performed at children's birthday parties as a juggler and clown.

Self-Referential:

RUDIMENTARY   basic (adj)

Synonyms:

Antonyms:

Context: Reading and writing are very **rudimentary** skills in everyday living.

Self-Referential:

RECUMBENT   lying down, resting (adj)

Synonyms:

Antonyms:

Context: Matisse painted several masterpieces showing **recumbent** figures.

Self-Referential:

BUTTRESS   a supporting piece of a structure (n), **or** to strengthen, support (v)

Synonyms:

Antonyms:

Context: The **buttresses** on the south side of the cathedral were deteriorating with age.

Yolanda attempted to **buttress** her argument with irrelevant considerations and personal attacks.

Self-Referential:

TRANSPOSE   to change from one place or mode to another (v)

Synonyms:

Antonyms:

Context: Gary needed to **transpose** the violin sonata so that he could play it on his cello.

Self-Referential:

PRACTICE SET 8

Instructions: Circle the answer that most closely approximates the definition of the word given.

1. **connive**   (A) sneak around   (B) lie   (C) hate   (D) secretly sympathize   (E) connect

2. **fabricate**   (A) create   (B) materialize   (C) make of cloth   (D) destroy   (E) remarkable

3. **rudimentary**   (A) vulgar   (B) reddish   (C) basic   (D) discourteous   (E) healthy

4. **viable**   (A) bridge   (B) oscillating   (C) excitable   (D) discernible   (E) workable

5. **burgeon**   (A) onus   (B) polish   (C) sprout   (D) flourish   (E) exaggeration

6. **ubiquitous**   (A) airy   (B) localized   (C) uplifting   (D) useful   (E) everywhere

7. **buttress**   (A) pillow   (B) support   (C) wall   (D) roof   (E) barricade

8. **fallow**   (A) false   (B) callous   (C) barren   (D) stammer   (E) imperfect

9. **bucolic**   (A) rustic   (B) sickly   (C) cow-like   (D) agitated   (E) beautiful

10. **recapitulate**   (A) re-surrender   (B) recover   (C) summarize   (D) relapse   (E) interchange

11. **dimension**   (A) depth   (B) deterioration   (C) decrease   (D) property of space   (E) quality of time

12. **nadir**   (A) zero   (B) important person   (C) zenith   (D) innocent   (E) low point

13. **susceptible**   (A) hanging   (B) prone   (C) supportive   (D) doubtful   (E) interrupted

14. **contiguous**   (A) moderate   (B) unified   (C) adjacent   (D) simultaneous   (E) conditional

15. **transpose**   (A) travel   (B) exceed   (C) copy   (D) change   (E) window

16. **proliferate**   (A) superfluous   (B) multiply   (C) corrupt   (D) diagram   (E) prepare

17. **synchronous**   (A) balanced   (B) logical   (C) flattering   (D) combined   (E) concurrent

18. **colossus**   (A) stadium   (B) cooperation   (C) arrangement   (D) huge thing   (E) major work

19. **incubation**   (A) seduction   (B) gestation   (C) accusation   (D) holding office   (E) burdened

20. **recalcitrant**   (A) stubborn   (B) retracting   (C) interchangeable   (D) honest   (E) restored

21. **rift** (A) float (B) musical improvisation (C) gap (D) wave (E) frost

22. **propensity** (A) inclination (B) force (C) procreation (D) preventative
(E) dullness

23. **tenuous** (A) sore (B) dark (C) restless (D) stiff (E) weak

24. **collaborate** (A) author (B) cooperate (C) relate (D) arrange (E) live together

25. **recumbent** (A) obligatory (B) superimposed (C) lying down
(D) refusing authority (E) righteous

26. **acculturate** (A) distill (B) ferment (C) amass (D) adapt (E) layer

88

PRACTICE SET 8
ANSWER KEY

1. D
2. A
3. C
4. E
5. D
6. E
7. B
8. C
9. A
10. C
11. D
12. E
13. B
14. C
15. D
16. B
17. E
18. D
19. B
20. A
21. C
22. A
23. E
24. B
25. C
26. D

FACADE   false front (n)

Synonyms:

Antonyms:

Context: His composure was merely a **facade**; inside he was actually grief-stricken.

Self-Referential:

PERIPHERAL outside, surrounding, auxiliary (adj)

Synonyms:

Antonyms:

Context: The church's youth group had a **peripheral** organization for junior teens.

Self-Referential:

NUCLEATE to cluster, to form a nucleus (v)

Synonyms:

Antonyms:

Context: The dust bunnies under the bed seem to **nucleate** until they become dust elephants.

Self-Referential:

STRATA layer (n)

Synonyms:

Antonyms:

Context: The archaeologists were working in the fifth **strata** beneath the ancient city.

Self-Referential:

LATERAL sideways, on the side (adj)

Synonyms:

Antonyms:

Context: Veronica made a **lateral** change in her position with the company, from one mid-management job to another.

Self-Referential:

90

AMORPHOUS   without shape, unclassifiable (adj)

Synonyms:

Antonyms:

Context: Grady held an **amorphous** position with the company, no one was quite sure what he did.

Self-Referential:

ELLIPSE   oval (n)

Synonyms:

Antonyms:

Context: Many scientists believe that Pluto's orbit around the sun is a more pronounced **ellipse** than Earth's.

Self-Referential:

TORTUOUS   twisty, winding, tricky (adj)

Synonyms:

Antonyms:

Context: The staircase carved into the cliff face was a **tortuous** climb, with many hazards along the way.

Self-Referential:

OBTUSE   difficult to understand, or unable to understand, stupid (adj)

Synonyms:

Antonyms:

Context: The history text was a particularly **obtuse** one, with extremely dense concepts.

Self-Referential:

STRIATE   to stripe (v)

Synonyms:

Antonyms:

Context: The massive floods would **striate** the banks of the river with debris and silt.

Self-Referential:

CONSTRICT   to compress, contract (v)

Synonyms:

Antonyms:

Context: When he tried to take the large pill, his throat felt as though it would **constrict** before he could swallow.

Self-Referential:

OCCLUDE   to obstruct, block up (v)

Synonyms:

Antonyms:

Context: The cave passage was **occluded** by the rubble left by the cave-in.

Self-Referential:

DORMANT   asleep, inactive (adj)

Synonyms:

Antonyms:

Context: The larvae of the seventeen-year cicada lie **dormant** underground for sixteen years, emerging in the seventeenth year to mate and lay eggs.

Self-Referential:

HALCYON happy, prosperous, peaceful (adj)

Synonyms:

Antonyms:

Context: Anna felt that the years she spent living and working in the north-western wilderness were the **halcyon** years of her life.

Self-Referential:

PLACID quiet, calm (adj)

Synonyms:

Antonyms:

Context: The waters of the lake were once again **placid** after the storm had passed.

Self-Referential:

STAGNANT stale, foul, motionless (adj)

Synonyms:

Antonyms:

Context: The water in the tidal pool became **stagnant** and smelly because of the unusually low tides.

Self-Referential:

ACCELERATE to speed up (v)

Synonyms:

Antonyms:

Context: Quincy decided to take an **accelerated** course of study so that he could graduate from college in three years instead of four.

Self-Referential:

PRECIPITATE   sudden or steep (adj), **or** to rain, snow, etc. **or** to bring about suddenly (v)

Synonyms:

Antonyms:

Context: On the road going down the side of the mountain, there was a particularly **precipitate** curve where many motorists went off the road.

The weather service claimed that there was no chance that it would **precipitate** today, yet it rained all afternoon.

Henry was worried that his actions would **precipitate** an extreme response from his co-workers.

Self-Referential:

SAUNTER   to walk in an easygoing swagger (v)

Synonyms:

Antonyms:

Context: Clint **sauntered** into the saloon with a belligerent look on his face.

Self-Referential:

AMBLE   to walk leisurely (v)

Synonyms:

Antonyms:

Context: Nancy and Chloe **ambled** along the park path, feeding the ducks and squirrels.

Self-Referential:

RECONNAISSANCE   a survey, esp. military action (n)

Synonyms:

Antonyms:

Context: My great-uncle Ralph earned a medal when he made a dangerous **reconnaissance** into enemy territory during World War II.

Self-Referential:

PULVERIZE   to smash into dust (v)

Synonyms:

Antonyms:

Context: The gravel had to be **pulverized** before it could be mixed into the concrete.

Self-Referential:

AVERT   to turn away, to avoid (v)

Synonyms:

Antonyms:

Context: Lydia tried to **avert** her eyes from the accident scene.

Self-Referential:

ERRANT   wandering, traveling (adj)

Synonyms:

Antonyms:

Context: Kyle spent four years as an **errant** missionary, traveling throughout Asia and the south Pacific.

Self-Referential:

CONVERGE   to come together, merge (v)

Synonyms:

Antonyms:

Context: Even though we know they remain parallel, the railroad tracks appear to **converge** on the horizon.

Self-Referential:

EGRESS   exit (n)

Synonyms:

Antonyms:

Context: As their fingers slipped on the smooth granite walls, the climbers be-
                       gan to realize there was no **egress** from the deep valley.

Self-Referential:

PRACTICE SET 9

Instructions: Circle the answer that most closely approximates the definition of the word given.

1. **constrict** (A) prohibit (B) compress (C) build (D) compel (E) interpret

2. **amble** (A) wander (B) attack (C) detour (D) walk slowly (E) sprint

3. **placid** (A) changeable (B) flat (C) calm (D) resinous (E) localized

4. **saunter** (A) gallop (B) fry (C) party (D) mistreat (E) swagger

5. **converge** (A) change (B) baptize (C) fall apart (D) come together (E) summon

6. **lateral** (A) sideways (B) secret (C) foregoing (D) praiseworthy (E) rising

7. **peripheral** (A) in front of (B) transient (C) surrounding (D) allowed (E) central

8. **precipitate** (A) shallow (B) forewarned (C) prepare (D) sudden (E) cloudy

9. **pulverize** (A) assault (B) lambaste (C) make loud noise (D) smash into dust (E) coat with dust

10. **strata** (A) opera (B) plan (C) prestige (D) inert (E) layer

11. **errant** (A) wandering (B) evil (C) conspicuous (D) small job (E) argumentative

12. **dormant** (A) mousy (B) inactive (C) on the back (D) sleepy (E) invigorated

13. **egress** (A) excess (B) entrance (C) excrete (D) exit (E) water bird

14. **tortuous** (A) painful (B) tormenting (C) apathetic (D) twisted (E) distortion

15. **accelerate** (A) accompany (B) speed up (C) approve (D) retard (E) condemn

16. **reconnaissance** (A) reawakening (B) conciliation (C) survey (D) redemption (E) recognition

17. **nucleate** (A) explode (B) cluster (C) fission (D) react (E) energize

18. **avert** (A) hate (B) affirm (C) turn away (D) testify (E) acknowledge

19. **amorphous** (A) shapeless (B) passionate (C) property transfer (D) vase-like (E) parallel

20. **occlude** (A) open up (B) flatten (C) conceal (D) inhabit (E) obstruct

21. **ellipse** (A) abbreviation (B) obscuring (C) circle (D) oval (E) orbit

22. **stagnant**   (A) motionless   (B) decomposed   (C) effluent   (D) old   (E) stumble

23. **striate**   (A) separate   (B) straight   (C) stripe   (D) affect   (E) assault

24. **facade**   (A) easy   (B) imitation   (C) prestige   (D) lining   (E) false front

25. **obtuse**   (A) triangular   (B) difficult   (C) fat   (D) unwieldy   (E) refractory

26. **halcyon**   (A) sleepy   (B) glowing   (C) healthy   (D) peaceful   (E) turbulent

98

PRACTICE SET 9
ANSWER KEY

LACTATE   to produce milk (v)

Synonyms:

Antonyms:

Context: Norris worried about his dog's ability to **lactate**, since the puppies
                  were not thriving.

Self-Referential:

SECRETE   to give off, **or** to hide (v)

Synonyms:

Antonyms:

Context: The skunk **secretes** a very smelly musk.

                           Perry tried to secrete a pistol in his briefcase.

Self-Referential:

WELTER   a chaotic mess (n)

Synonyms:

Antonyms:

Context: Amid a **welter** of competing interests, Elisa found herself more and
                           more confused.

Self-Referential:

CYCLICAL   periodic and repeating (adj)

Synonyms:

Antonyms:

Context: Because of the **cyclical** nature of the tides, the harbormaster was re-
                           luctant to allow the large ship to dock.

Self-Referential:

TEPID   lukewarm, room temperature (adj)

Synonyms:

Antonyms:

Context: Because he had let it sit out for several hours, Charles' coffee was
                           tepid.

Self-Referential:

LUMINOUS   glowing, lighted (adj)

Synonyms:

Antonyms:

Context: The bride seemed **luminous** as she walked up the aisle.

Self-Referential:

MURKY   cloudy, not clear (adj)

Synonyms:

Antonyms:

Context: After the little boys dumped mud into the wading pool, the water was **murky**.

Self-Referential:

TRANSLUCENT   allowing light to pass through but not transparent (adj)

Synonyms:

Antonyms:

Context: The stained-glass windows were wonderfully **translucent** after they were thoroughly cleaned.

Self-Referential:

ENCUMBER   to burden (v)

Synonyms:

Antonyms:

Context: His irresponsible actions only served to **encumber** his parents with excessive debt.

Self-Referential:

IMPERMEABLE   not porous, not allowing flow-through (adj)

Synonyms:

Antonyms:

Context: The lining of the landfill must be **impermeable**, so that toxic substances will not leak through.

Self-Referential:

CALLOUS   hardened, unsympathetic (adj)

Synonyms:

Antonyms:

Context: The politician did not want to appear **callous** toward the plight of the earthquake victims.

Self-Referential:

ELASTICITY   adaptability, springiness (n)

Synonyms:

Antonyms:

Context: A toddler has a surprising amount of **elasticity** when it comes to a changing living situation.

Self-Referential:

TRACTABLE   controllable, cooperative (adj)

Synonyms:

Antonyms:

Context: As a group, the students were not very **tractable**, but individually the dean was able to get them to change their position.

Self-Referential:

PIGMENT   coloring element in paint (n)

Synonyms:

Antonyms:

Context: Marvin had a difficult time matching the **pigment** in the old paint
                        with the newer brands.

Self-Referential:

SPECTRUM   the range of all colors, complete range (n)

Synonyms:

Antonyms:

Context: The drama encompassed the entire **spectrum** of human emotion,
                        from love to hate and from anxiety to serenity.

Self-Referential:

FLORID   flowery, **or** reddish (adj)

Synonyms:

Antonyms:

Context: Shelley's new linens had a **florid** design, with cabbage roses and
                        lilies predominating.

                        Eric's face was **florid** with excitement.

Self-Referential:

IRIDESCENT   having shiny rainbow colors, shimmery (adj)

Synonyms:

Antonyms:

Context: The oil slick was **iridescent** as it reflected the light on the water.

Self-Referential:

MOSAIC a picture made of many small parts such as tiles (n)

Synonyms:

Antonyms:

Context: On the floor of the main hall was a **mosaic** of the university seal, made from local marble.

Self-Referential:

PIED multi-colored and blotchy (adj)

Synonyms:

Antonyms:

Context: When she came down with the measles, her face was **pied** with roseola rash.

Self-Referential:

STIPPLE to speckle or fleck, esp. with paint (v), **or** the effect of many small dots (n)

Synonyms:

Antonyms:

Context: Seurat was famous for **stippling** the canvas to create his unique effect.

His paintings were prime examples of **stipple** taken to its highest degree of artistry.

Self-Referential:

TRANSCENDENTAL abstract, supernatural (adj)

Synonyms:

Antonyms:

Context: She believed that the prohibition against murder was both universal and **transcendental**, having a place in every human society, and therefore ordained by God.

Self-Referential:

IMPALPABLE   not physical, not able to be touched (adj)

Synonyms:

Antonyms:

Context: John Kennedy's charisma, although **impalpable**, can still be conveyed through the medium of old film footage.

Self-Referential:

MONOLITH   a single, huge structure, or a large organization acting as one force (n)

Synonyms:

Antonyms:

Context: The mega-corporation was viewed by outsiders as an impenetrable **monolith**.

Self-Referential:

HYDRATE   to add water to (v)

Synonyms:

Antonyms:

Context: To **hydrate** the chemical compound would cause an explosive reaction.

Self-Referential:

EMOLLIENT   lotion that moisturizes (n)

Synonyms:

Antonyms:

Context: After spending the day at sea, Jessica needed to apply some **emollient** to her face.

Self-Referential:

FERROUS   with iron (adj)

Synonyms:

Antonyms:

Context: The **ferrous** deposits in the region made it difficult to navigate with a compass.

Self-Referential:

PRACTICE SET 10

Instructions: Circle the answer that most closely approximates the definition of the word given.

1. **murky** (A) deep (B) cloudy (C) quiet (D) tranquil (E) clear

2. **pied** (A) round (B) humored (C) splotchy (D) hampered (E) inquired

3. **elasticity** (A) stretchiness (B) good-naturedness (C) moodiness (D) rigidity (E) firmness

4. **pigment** (A) small hog (B) coloring (C) small person (D) hue (E) paint

5. **hydrate** (A) water source (B) pipe (C) mythological monster (D) sea creature (E) add water to

6. **secrete** (A) confidence (B) dissent (C) region (D) hide (E) safety

7. **transcendental** (A) religious (B) pious (C) traditional (D) interpretive (E) supernatural

8. **tepid** (A) cool (B) lukewarm (C) unbearably hot (D) frozen (E) cold

9. **welter** (A) scar (B) abrasion (C) jumble (D) defaulter (E) sweater

10. **iridescent** (A) glossy (B) showy (C) oily (D) rainbow-like (E) glowing

11. **ferrous** (A) animal-like (B) searching (C) savage (D) containing protein (E) containing iron

12. **spectrum** (A) theorization (B) range (C) ghost (D) illusion (E) format

13. **callous** (A) hard (B) immature (C) ignorant (D) cruel (E) tumor

14. **monolith** (A) monument (B) cenotaph (C) small stone (D) single structure (E) monster

15. **impermeable** (A) transient (B) not porous (C) impulsive (D) unwilling (E) implacable

16. **florid** (A) perplexed (B) flowery (C) disproved (D) boat (E) coin

17. **lactate** (A) sweat (B) lay eggs (C) make cheese (D) make milk (E) make butter

18. **impalpable** (A) unfeeling (B) supernatural (C) immaterial (D) physical (E) neutral

19. **tractable** (A) uncontrollable (B) pliant (C) towable (D) implacable (E) mappable

20. **cyclical** (A) periodic (B) missive (C) pessimistic (D) tumescent (E) island-like

21. **emollient** (A) appointment (B) lotion (C) hysterical (D) pacifier (E) alleviator

22. **mosaic** (A) set of laws (B) ambling (C) picture (D) turtle (E) moss-covered

23. **luminous** (A) famous (B) happy (C) sunny (D) clumsy (E) glowing

24. **encumber** (A) vegetable (B) ponder (C) meet (D) besiege (E) burden

25. **translucent** (A) semitransparent (B) thick (C) changeable (D) permeating (E) moving

26. **stipple** (A) beard growth (B) condition (C) dot (D) stripe (E) shape

PRACTICE SET 10
ANSWER KEY

1. B
2. C
3. A
4. B
5. E
6. D
7. E
8. B
9. C
10. D
11. E
12. B
13. A
14. D
15. B
16. B
17. D
18. C
19. B
20. A
21. B
22. C
23. E
24. E
25. A
26. C

TURBID   muddy, obscured (adj)

Synonyms:

Antonyms:

Context: The **turbid** waters of the flooded creek made it difficult for the fishermen to see any fish.

Self-Referential:

ARID   dry (adj)

Synonyms:

Antonyms:

Context: The soil in the plant pots had become completely **arid** from neglect.

Self-Referential:

AERATE   to supply or combine with oxygen or air (v)

Synonyms:

Antonyms:

Context: The egg whites are **aerated** until they are stiff when one makes meringue.

Self-Referential:

RESUSCITATE   to revive, renew (v)

Synonyms:

Antonyms:

Context: Trevor attempted to **resuscitate** the failing business, but no one was interested in buying used widgets.

Self-Referential:

CARRION   animal remains (n)

Synonyms:

Antonyms:

Context: The buzzards circled around the **carrion** until traffic was light enough to let them land and dine.

Self-Referential:

DEMISE   death, cessation (n)

Synonyms:

Antonyms:

Context: The **demise** of his aunt did not stop Manny from moving to Ohio.

Self-Referential:

VAPID   uninteresting, without liveliness (adj)

Synonyms:

Antonyms:

Context: He was probably the most **vapid** entertainer she had ever laid eyes on.

Self-Referential:

CLOYING   sweet, sentimental (adj)

Synonyms:

Antonyms:

Context: The smell of the perfume shop was **cloying** and overwhelming.

Self-Referential:

PUNGENT   strong tasting or smelling (adj)

Synonyms:

Antonyms:

Context: The new Tex-Mex restaurant has a great salsa that is **pungent** and tasty.

Self-Referential:

REDOLENT aromatic, having an odor (adj)

Synonyms:

Antonyms:

Context: The forest was **redolent** of pine needles and other woodsy smells.

Self-Referential:

OSTENSIBLE apparent, under a pretext (adj)

Synonyms:

Antonyms:

Context: The structure was an **ostensible** storefront, but in reality it was a speakeasy.

Self-Referential:

DISCORD argument, strife (n)

Synonyms:

Antonyms:

Context: Whenever he came to visit, Uncle Rupert caused **discord** and family quarrels.

Self-Referential:

FATUOUS foolish, silly (adj)

Synonyms:

Antonyms:

Context: The campers were being foolhardy in their **fatuous** disregard for danger from the swollen stream.

Self-Referential:

INANE   silly, empty-headed (adj)

Synonyms:

Antonyms:

Context: Lloyd certainly has some **inane** ideas about what to do on a date.

Self-Referential:

LUDICROUS   ridiculous, absurd (adj)

Synonyms:

Antonyms:

Context: The idea that Mother Theresa is in her line of work for the money is **ludicrous** in the extreme.

Self-Referential:

DILETTANTE   amateur, dabbler (n)

Synonyms:

Antonyms:

Context: When it comes to music, Bartholomew is a mere **dilettante**, while Ken is a professional.

Self-Referential:

COGITATE   to think hard, ponder (v)

Synonyms:

Antonyms:

Context: Ursula needed plenty of time in order to **cogitate** and come up with a decision about her marriage.

Self-Referential:

FORAGE   to look for food (v)

Synonyms:

Antonyms:

Context: Lester went to **forage** in the refrigerator because he was extremely hungry.

Self-Referential:

PERUSE   to study thoroughly (v)

Synonyms:

Antonyms:

Context: Frank intended to **peruse** the entire economics textbook, in order to prepare for his exam.

Self-Referential:

PERSPICACIOUS   keen, mentally sharp (adj)

Synonyms:

Antonyms:

Context: After waking up early and eating a good breakfast, Jim felt particularly **perspicacious** and ready for school.

Self-Referential:

DOCTRINE   creed, belief (n)

Synonyms:

Antonyms:

Context: Some of the early American sects held the **doctrine** that musical instruments were evil.

Self-Referential:

NAIVETE　　　　　　unsophisticatedness, artlessness (adj)

Synonyms:

Antonyms:

Context:　　　　　　　Heather displayed an unusual degree of **naivete** when confronted with her wrongdoings.

Self-Referential:

BELIE　　　　　　　to contradict, to give false cover to (v)

Synonyms:

Antonyms:

Context:　　　　　　　Her smiling face **belied** the fact that she felt devastated and grief-stricken.

Self-Referential:

IMPLAUSIBLE　　　not believable (adj)

Synonyms:

Antonyms:

Context:　　　　　　　The story Honoria made up about her whereabouts last night was totally **implausible**.

Self-Referential:

PONTIFICAL　　　　like a pontiff, a pope, extremely authoritative (adj)

Synonyms:

Antonyms:

Context:　　　　　　　Gilbert was given to making **pontifical** pronouncements to his employees.

Self-Referential:

FALTER   to stumble, hesitate (v)

Synonyms:

Antonyms:

Context: **The actor did not falter or miss a single cue throughout the entire play.**

Self-Referential:

PRACTICE SET 11

Instructions: Circle the answer that most closely approximates the definition of the word given.

1. **carrion** (A) decomposition (B) animal cargo (C) animal remains (D) animal excrement (E) foulness

2. **pungent** (A) perforate (B) scholarly (C) retaliatory (D) strong (E) cleaning agent

3. **inane** (A) crazy (B) silly (C) happy (D) blessed (E) innocent

4. **cogitate** (A) twist (B) rotate gears (C) speak out (D) exist (E) think

5. **doctrine** (A) belief (B) medicine (C) apostasy (D) tolerance (E) theory

6. **fatuous** (A) obese (B) ridiculous (C) hearty (D) serious (E) mournful

7. **perspicacious** (A) sweaty (B) surly (C) obtuse (D) keen (E) outlook

8. **arid** (A) clean (B) deserted (C) fertile (D) affectionate (E) dry

9. **ostensible** (A) appealing (B) overt (C) actual (D) apparent (E) erroneous

10. **belie** (A) a falsehood (B) creed (C) disparage (D) lead (E) contradict

11. **discord** (A) change (B) disagreement (C) unity (D) lecture (E) inform

12. **peruse** (A) examine (B) agitate (C) skim over (D) summarize (E) digest

13. **pontifical** (A) cape-like (B) overly authoritative (C) blessed (D) considered (E) substantial

14. **resuscitate** (A) inflate (B) revive (C) make younger (D) renascent (E) stifle

15. **implausible** (A) unbelievable (B) imprudent (C) important (D) believable (E) likely

16. **ludicrous** (A) worthwhile (B) silly (C) intelligible (D) slippery (E) money-grubbing

17. **forage** (A) advance (B) search (C) abstain (D) energy (E) raid

18. **cloying** (A) sentimental (B) earthy (C) prosaic (D) confined (E) bitter

19. **aerate** (A) flatten (B) fly (C) make green (D) mix with air (E) nest

20. **falter** (A) change (B) harness (C) stumble (D) stride (E) affirm

21. **naivete** (A) experience (B) artlessness (C) worldliness (D) tastefulness (E) sophistication

22. **redolent**   (A) rolling   (B) forgetful   (C) lazy   (D) aromatic   (E) resounding

23. **demise**   (A) rebirth   (B) death   (C) oust   (D) lament   (E) continuation

24. **dilettante**   (A) amateur   (B) generalist   (C) student   (D) professional   (E) expert

25. **vapid**   (A) happy   (B) uninteresting   (C) stimulating   (D) sexy   (E) strong

26. **turbid**   (A) muddy   (B) clear   (C) distended   (D) bombastic   (E) degenerate

PRACTICE SET 11
ANSWER KEY

1. C
2. D
3. B
4. E
5. A
6. B
7. D
8. E
9. D
10. E
11. B
12. A
13. B
14. B
15. A
16. B
17. B
18. A
19. D
20. C
21. B
22. D
23. B
24. A
25. B
26. A

RELIC   a remnant, a souvenir, a venerated object (n)

Synonyms:

Antonyms:

Context: The pennants and posters were **relics** of Charles's days as a college
                      football player.

Self-Referential:

JUGGERNAUT   a large vehicle that crushes anything in its path (n)

Synonyms:

Antonyms:

Context: Gwendolyn was like a **juggernaut** in her desire for success and
                       fame, she did not let anyone get in her way.

Self-Referential:

PROSCRIBE   to condemn, to forbid (v)

Synonyms:

Antonyms:

Context: Some people feel it is archaic for the church to **proscribe** divorce.

Self-Referential:

CENSURE   to disapprove, condemn, **or** disapproval, condemnation (v, n)

Synonyms:

Antonyms:

Context: The school board voted to **censure** the wayward teacher.
                       Martin could not bear the **censure** he felt from his parents.

Self-Referential:

IMPUNITY   without fear of punishment (n)

Synonyms:

Antonyms:

Context: George knew he could spend his friend's money with **impunity**.

Self-Referential:

INDICTMENT   formal charge against a person (n)

Synonyms:

Antonyms:

Context: The grand jury handed down an **indictment** against the mobster, charging him with racketeering and extortion.

Self-Referential:

GOURMAND   one who likes to eat a lot (n)

Synonyms:

Antonyms:

Context: The restaurant offered an all-you-can-eat menu, and was overwhelmed by hungry **gourmands**.

Self-Referential:

ASCETIC   austere, disciplined (adj)

Synonyms:

Antonyms:

Context: The lifestyle at the monastery was extremely **ascetic,** without many worldly pleasures.

Self-Referential:

HEDONIST   one who lives for pleasure (n)

Synonyms:

Antonyms:

Context: The island paradise was populated with **hedonists**, who enjoyed the pleasures of the senses.

Self-Referential:

PROFLIGATE   extravagant, prodigal (adj)

Synonyms:

Antonyms:

Context: It is unwise to be so **profligate** with your savings; you should keep it for a rainy day.

Self-Referential:

OBDURATE   stubborn, unfeeling (adj)

Synonyms:

Antonyms:

Context: With respect to the besotted young swain's amorous feelings, Camille was completely **obdurate**, she had no feelings for him at all.

Self-Referential:

ALTRUISM   unselfish behavior (n)

Synonyms:

Antonyms:

Context: There are few examples of **altruism** anymore; most people seem to be motivated by self-interest.

Self-Referential:

QUISLING   traitor (n)

Synonyms:

Antonyms:

Context: Henry was considered a **quisling** by his football club for giving information to their rivals.

Self-Referential:

VERACITY   truthfulness (n)

Synonyms:

Antonyms:

Context: She could not be sure of his story's **veracity**, after all, he had lied so many times before.

Self-Referential:

PROBITY   honesty (n)

Synonyms:

Antonyms:

Context: The scientist conducted the controversial tests with **probity** and scientific rigor.

Self-Referential:

CANDOR   straightforwardness, sincerity (n)

Synonyms:

Antonyms:

Context: Norman knew he could treat them with the utmost **candor** because they were used to unveiled truthfulness.

Self-Referential:

ARTLESSNESS   crudeness, naturalness (n)

Synonyms:

Antonyms:

Context: The **artlessness** of young children is unattractive in teenagers or adults.

Self-Referential:

VITUPERATE   to scold with excessively harsh language (v)

Synonyms:

Antonyms:

Context: When the child spilled her chocolate milk, her father lost his temper and began to **vituperate**.

Self-Referential:

TIRADE   a long, harsh, highly critical speech (n)

Synonyms:

Antonyms:

Context: Chester began his tedious **tirade** against everything the government did.

Self-Referential:

REPROBATE   depraved, condemned (adj)

Synonyms:

Antonyms:

Context: He was a **reprobate** thief and a violent criminal.

Self-Referential:

CULPABLE   deserving of blame (adj)

Synonyms:

Antonyms:

Context: The court found that Manny was not **culpable** for the crime because he was legally insane.

Self-Referential:

CASTIGATE   to scold severely (v)

Synonyms:

Antonyms:

Context: Lyle was prepared to be **castigated** for the failure of his plan.

Self-Referential:

COUNTENANCE   face, expression, **or** to allow to happen (n, v)

Synonyms:

Antonyms:

Context: Her **countenance** was doleful, she was overcome with sadness.
Kelly could not **countenance** the illicit activities taking place in the office.

Self-Referential:

APPROBATION   praise, approval (n)

Synonyms:

Antonyms:

Context: Jeanna's new compositions were met with **approbation** and delight.

Self-Referential:

ADULATION   admiration (n)

Synonyms:

Antonyms:

Context: The teenager's **adulation** for the rock star was excessive, knowing no limits on souvenirs, albums, and tee-shirts.

Self-Referential:

PRACTICE SET 12

Instructions: Circle the answer that most closely approximates the definition of the word given.

1. **artlessness**   (A) sterility   (B) crudeness   (C) bareness   (D) slyness   (E) innocence

2. **altruism**   (A) socialism   (B) truthfulness   (C) selfishness   (D) avarice   (E) selflessness

3. **countenance**   (A) condone   (B) clock   (C) sorrow   (D) enumeration   (E) burden

4. **indictment**   (A) accusation   (B) indoctrination   (C) prevalence   (D) investigation   (E) formal charge

5. **reprobate**   (A) rebuked   (B) depraved   (C) sly   (D) rakish   (E) libertine

6. **relic**   (A) bagatelle   (B) appendage   (C) venerated object   (D) pillar   (E) artifact

7. **adulation**   (A) maturation   (B) mockery   (C) admiration   (D) majority   (E) knowledge

8. **hedonist**   (A) huckster   (B) one who seeks warmth   (C) one who seeks pleasure   (D) complainer   (E) deviant

9. **censure**   (A) prohibit   (B) condemn   (C) dislike   (D) fear   (E) bowdlerize

10. **castigate**   (A) emasculate   (B) scatter   (C) scold   (D) approve   (E) plaster

11. **profligate**   (A) multiply   (B) expensive   (C) silly   (D) extravagant   (E) profitable

12. **tirade**   (A) military march   (B) despotic ruler   (C) exhaustive list   (D) hypocrisy   (E) harsh speech

13. **juggernaut**   (A) one who travels   (B) one who juggles   (C) inexorable vehicle   (D) runaway truck   (E) malapropism

14. **veracity**   (A) dearness   (B) common usage   (C) extremism   (D) pointlessness   (E) truthfulness

15. **approbation**   (A) valuation   (B) evaluation   (C) praise   (D) engagement   (E) condemnation

16. **gourmand**   (A) trencherman   (B) connoisseur   (C) food expert   (D) bulimic   (E) sous chef

17. **vituperate**   (A) drink   (B) visualize   (C) praise highly   (D) scold harshly   (E) bite

18. **obdurate**   (A) outrageous   (B) dense   (C) stubborn   (D) apparent   (E) divided

19. **culpable**   (A) blameworthy   (B) conspiratorial   (C) sortable   (D) praiseworthy
(E) innocent

20. **proscribe**   (A) recommend medicine   (B) forbid   (C) write by hand
(D) allocate   (E) enable

21. **candor**   (A) fearlessness   (B) dishonesty   (C) frankness   (D) piety
(E) deviousness

22. **impunity**   (A) polluting agent   (B) honesty   (C) blasphemy   (D) denial
(E) without fear of punishment

23. **ascetic**   (A) sterile   (B) acid   (C) pure   (D) august   (E) austere

24. **quisling**   (A) idealist   (B) small animal   (C) game show participant   (D) loyalist
(E) traitor

25. **probity**   (A) inquisitiveness   (B) honesty   (C) judgment   (D) probability
(E) factuality

PRACTICE SET 12
ANSWER KEY

1. B
2. E
3. A
4. E
5. B
6. C
7. C
8. C
9. B
10. C
11. D
12. E
13. C
14. E
15. C
16. A
17. D
18. C
19. A
20. B
21. C
22. E
23. E
24. E
25. B

TRAVESTY   mockery, parody (n)

Synonyms:

Antonyms:

Context: The obviously racially biased decision was a **travesty** of justice.

Self-Referential:

DERISION   scorning, ridicule (n)

Synonyms:

Antonyms:

Context: Scott could no longer bear the **derision** of the crowd, so he quit baseball.

Self-Referential:

VINDICTIVE vengeful, spiteful (adj)

Synonyms:

Antonyms:

Context: Allison's ongoing criticism of Reggie was becoming merely **vindictive**.

Self-Referential:

TRUCULENT ferocious, extremely harsh (adj)

Synonyms:

Antonyms:

Context: The review not only panned the movie, it was downright **truculent** in its blasting of the quality of the acting.

Self-Referential:

AFFABLE friendly, pleasant (adj)

Synonyms:

Antonyms:

Context: My grandfather has an **affable** smile to go with his sweet disposition.

Self-Referential:

URBANE sophisticated, worldly (adj)

Synonyms:

Antonyms:

Context: She had a very **urbane** air about her, with her fashionable clothes and her witty conversation.

Self-Referential:

LIONIZE   to make much of (v)

Synonyms:

Antonyms:

Context: Yolanda was **lionized** by the local people.

Self-Referential:

AGGRANDIZE   to praise greatly, to make seem greater (v)

Synonyms:

Antonyms:

Context: Bernard had a great talent for **aggrandizing** his accomplishments.

Self-Referential:

EFFRONTERY   boldness (n)

Synonyms:

Antonyms:

Context: The shy child could not be accused of **effrontery**, he was always extremely polite.

Self-Referential:

GRANDILOQUENT   having high-sounding speech (adj)

Synonyms:

Antonyms:

Context: Phil made a **grandiloquent** plea for saving the watershed.

Self-Referential:

SPURIOUS false, fraudulent (adj)

Synonyms:

Antonyms:

Context: Keith made **spurious** claims about his ability to work with computers.

Self-Referential:

TIMOROUS timid, fearful (adj)

Synonyms:

Antonyms:

Context: The **timorous** mouse ran from the ferocious cat.

Self-Referential:

REDOUBTABLE formidable, illustrious (adj)

Synonyms:

Antonyms:

Context: The **redoubtable** personage of Queen Victoria made her mark in literature as well as history and the arts.

Self-Referential:

AESTHETIC artistic, relating to beauty (adj)

Synonyms:

Antonyms:

Context: The general consensus was that the new building was lacking in **aesthetic** quality, being in the shape of a cracker box.

Self-Referential:

UNPREPOSSESSING   homely, plain (adj)

Synonyms:

Antonyms:

Context: The seaside cottage was **unprepossessing**, tucked away among the dunes.

Self-Referential:

TENTATIVE   hesitant, uncertain (adj)

Synonyms:

Antonyms:

Context: The baby made a few **tentative** steps across the playpen.

Self-Referential:

DISCREET   having good judgment, prudent (adj)

Synonyms:

Antonyms:

Context: Vanessa was not very **discreet** in her decision to publish her unexpurgated memoirs.

Self-Referential:

DAUNT   to subdue or tame (v)

Synonyms:

Antonyms:

Context: Ogden would not be **daunted** by his detractors.

Self-Referential:

SOLICITUDE   over-attentive care, anxiety (n)

Synonyms:

Antonyms:

Context: The **solicitude** with which she nursed her mother went unappreci-
ated.

Self-Referential:

DISQUIET   to disturb, upset (v)

Synonyms:

Antonyms:

Context: After seeing the horror movie, Jane was **disquieted** by every little
sound.

Self-Referential:

COMMODIOUS   having ample space (adj)

Synonyms:

Antonyms:

Context: The new car was more than **commodious**, it had room for the whole
family.

Self-Referential:

EXACERBATE   to aggravate, make worse (v)

Synonyms:

Antonyms:

Context: The bureaucratic red tape only served to **exacerbate** the problems
associated with registering for classes.

Self-Referential:

CONTRITE   sorry, repentant (adj)

Synonyms:

Antonyms:

Context: Zach was not very **contrite** after pushing the other little boys down.

Self-Referential:

LEVITY   lightness, good humor (n)

Synonyms:

Antonyms:

Context: The professor tried to inject some **levity** into her lecture by making lame jokes.

Self-Referential:

QUERULOUS   complaining, whining (adj)

Synonyms:

Antonyms:

Context: The **querulous** child frequently got what she wanted by throwing tantrums.

Self-Referential:

PIQUE   offense, resentment, **or** to provoke or excite (n, v)

Synonyms:

Antonyms:

Context: She stormed off in a fit of **pique**.
The movie preview **piqued** my interest.

Self-Referential:

PRACTICE SET 13

Instructions: Circle the answer that most closely approximates the definition of the word given.

1. **solicitude** (A) loneliness (B) salesmanship (C) cheerfulness (D) over-attentive care (E) prostitution

2. **aggrandize** (A) glorify (B) humiliate (C) irritate (D) grandiose (E) measure

3. **unprepossessing** (A) not previously owned (B) humble (C) extroverted (D) loquacious (E) having good qualities

4. **contrite** (A) opposed (B) feeble (C) sorry (D) meritorious (E) invalid

5. **truculent** (A) extremely harsh (B) stubborn (C) brash (D) snide (E) pouty

6. **pique** (A) apex (B) offense (C) fairy (D) bland (E) fit

7. **spurious** (A) goading (B) false (C) slick (D) enticing (E) sarcastic

8. **travesty** (A) wall hanging (B) sad drama (C) mockery (D) idiosyncrasy (E) weaving

9. **commodious** (A) cramped (B) helpful (C) meek (D) loud (E) roomy

10. **affable** (A) humorous (B) friendly (C) amorous (D) supercilious (E) derogatory

11. **discreet** (A) contained (B) uncouth (C) rash (D) prudent (E) quiet

12. **timorous** (A) timid (B) awkward (C) noisy (D) chiming (E) bashful

13. **querulous** (A) curious (B) sad (C) fighting (D) whining (E) making inquiry

14. **effrontery** (A) fearfulness (B) timidity (C) snobbishness (D) boldness (E) profanity

15. **derision** (A) scowling (B) unhappiness (C) scorn (D) falsehood (E) entanglement

16. **exacerbate** (A) make acidic (B) mold (C) make worse (D) exemplify (E) ridicule

17. **redoubtable** (A) certain (B) reconsider (C) uncertain (D) formidable (E) meek

18. **disquiet** (A) loud (B) disturb (C) make noise (D) hinder (E) baffle

19. **urbane** (A) sophisticated (B) relaxed (C) calm (D) of a city (E) hurried

20. **daunt** (A) make unsure (B) make comfortable (C) hold steady (D) upset (E) subdue

21. **grandiloquent** (A) large (B) fluent (C) facile (D) having lofty speech (E) lengthy speech

22. **vindictive** (A) justified (B) wine-like (C) angry (D) vengeful (E) petty

23. **tentative** (A) certain (B) unhesitating (C) temporary (D) wobbly (E) hesitant

24. **aesthetic** (A) clean (B) unconscious (C) relating to medicine (D) relating to beauty (E) relating to art

25. **levity** (A) priestliness (B) heaviness (C) good humor (D) ponderous (E) serpentine

26. **lionize** (A) roar (B) show leadership (C) take the larger share (D) belittle (E) make much of

138

PRACTICE SET 13
ANSWER KEY

1. D
2. A
3. B
4. C
5. A
6. B
7. B
8. C
9. E
10. B
11. D
12. A
13. D
14. D
15. C
16. C
17. D
18. B
19. A
20. E
21. D
22. D
23. E
24. D
25. C
26. E

INTUITIVE   known through immediate insight not gained through rational thought (adj)

Synonyms:

Antonyms:

Context: He has always had an **intuitive** distrust of opinion polls.

Self-Referential:

SYBIL   witch (n)

Synonyms:

Antonyms:

Context: Although Caroline is not a sorceress, there is about her something suggestive of the **sybil**.

Self-Referential:

METICULOUS   extremely careful, fastidious (adj)

Synonyms:

Antonyms:

Context: The zoo attendant took **meticulous** pains to bathe the porcupines daily.

Self-Referential:

PRESCIENCE   the ability to foretell events (n)

Synonyms:

Antonyms:

Context: The traveler's **prescience** caused him to avoid Miami during hurricane season.

Self-Referential:

INTELLIGIBLE   understandable, comprehensible (adj)

Synonyms:

Antonyms:

Context: Unless you can give me an **intelligible** account of your work, you will not be promoted.

Self-Referential:

LIMPID   clear, serene, transparent (adj)

Synonyms:

Antonyms:

Context: The deep blue of her eyes made them seem like **limpid** pools.

Self-Referential:

INADVERTENCE   oversight, unwittingness (n)

Synonyms:

Antonyms:

Context: It was through the company's **inadvertence** that the pet alligator was shipped to Alaska rather than to Florida.

Self-Referential:

CONCEDE   to yield, to grant (v)

Synonyms:

Antonyms:

Context: Though she **conceded** that even English teachers make mistakes, the dean could not excuse the English professor's bad grammar.

Self-Referential:

RETRACT   to take back, recant

Synonyms:

Antonyms:

Context: Dr. Jones would not **retract** his statement that the initials Ph.D. mean 'probably half dead.'

Self-Referential:

IDEOLOGY   a set of beliefs (n)

Synonyms:

Antonyms:

Context: A strong distrust of religious authority was behind all of the pastor's **ideologies**.

Self-Referential:

TEMPERAMENT   disposition, sensibility (n)

Synonyms:

Antonyms:

Context: Because his employer did not believe Thomas had the **temperament** to be a teacher, he would not permit the man to join the faculty.

Self-Referential:

PEER   an equal (n)

Synonyms:

Antonyms:

Context: Despite his faulty hearing, Beethoven has had no **peer** as a composer.

Self-Referential:

CHAUVINIST   extreme patriot, one who believes one's group is superior to another

Synonyms:

Antonyms:

Context: Just because he waves flags whenever he speaks, Senator Foghorn should not be regarded as a **chauvinist**.

Self-Referential:

CONTEND   to fight with, oppose (v)

Synonyms:

Antonyms:

Context: It is inadvisable to **contend** with lawyers about the fairness of legal fees.

Self-Referential:

SCRUPLE   to have moral qualms about, **or** a moral principle

Synonyms:

Antonyms:

Context: I do not **scruple** to advise persons with leprosy to seek medical aid. The clergyman had **scruples** about any discussions of abortion.

Self-Referential:

CONCUR   to agree (v)

Synonyms:

Antonyms:

Context: The two candidates **concurred** in their belief that young voters should not be paid to cast their ballots.

Self-Referential:

PRATTLE   to babble, as a child (v)

Synonyms:

Antonyms:

Context: The impatient parents grew tired of their child's **prattle** at three in the morning.

Self-Referential:

OBLIVIOUS   unknowing, unheeding (adj)

Synonyms:

Antonyms:

Context: The umpire was **oblivious** of the pitcher's behavior in wetting his thumb on a sponge attached to his belt.

Self-Referential:

ARCANE   secret, esoteric (adj)

Synonyms:

Antonyms:

Context: The **arcane** knowledge of ancient magic led the astrologer to startling conclusions.

Self-Referential:

CONUNDRUM   a riddle, puzzle (n)

Synonyms:

Antonyms:

Context: It was Newton who finally explained the **conundrum** of falling apples.

Self-Referential:

ALLUSIVE   referring to or hinting at something, esp. in literature (adj)

Synonyms:

Antonyms:

Context: The students grew weary of the **allusive** quotations in the professor's learned lectures.

Self-Referential:

ELUCIDATE　　　　to make clear, explain (v)

Synonyms:

Antonyms:

Context:　　　　I hope you will **elucidate** your wild statements about the behavior of teenagers.

Self-Referential:

FLAGRANT　　　　bold, open, apparent (adj)

Synonyms:

Antonyms:

Context:　　　　The preacher's habit of smoking cigars while delivering sermons was in **flagrant** violation of the city's safety regulations.

Self-Referential:

SALIENT　　　　noticeable, prominent (adj)

Synonyms:

Antonyms:

Context:　　　　Constant references to family unity were **salient** features of the politician's speeches.

Self-Referential:

ERUDITION　　　　knowledge, esp. gained from books (n)

Synonyms:

Antonyms:

Context:　　　　A good history writer should not laden her work with excessive displays of **erudition**.

Self-Referential:

PROCTOR   one who supervises students at an exam (n)

Synonyms:

Antonyms:

Context: An honorable student is usually offended by the presence of **proc-tors** at examinations.

Self-Referential:

PRACTICE SET 14

Instructions: Circle the answer that most closely approximates the definition of the word given.

1. **limpid** (A) saccharine (B) clear (C) injured (D) circulatory (E) limber

2. **conundrum** (A) obvious statement (B) transition (C) riddle (D) conjunction
    (E) loud noise

3. **intuitive** (A) illogical (B) surprising (C) given to guesswork (D) observing
    (E) known through insight

4. **prescience** (A) immediacy (B) foreknowledge (C) soon-to-come
    (D) mistakenness (E) illogicality

5. **prattle** (A) talk endlessly (B) preach (C) behave mischievously (D) babble
    (E) gibber

6. **arcane** (A) curved (B) esoteric (C) covered (D) open (E) ancient

7. **allusive** (A) referring to (B) deceptive (C) abusive (D) loud (E) ill-mannered

8. **elucidate** (A) dodge logically (B) speak clearly (C) make clear (D) becloud
    (E) evade

9. **oblivious** (A) effacing (B) unknowing (C) duty-bound (D) indirect
    (E) knowledgeable

10. **sybil** (A) brother or sister (B) saint (C) politeness (D) graceful woman (E) witch

11. **intelligible** (A) intellectual (B) meaningless (C) expressive (D) purposeful
    (E) understandable

12. **concede** (A) yield (B) show self-importance (C) hide (D) deny a truth
    (E) form an idea

13. **scruple** (A) economize (B) carelessness (C) show moral compunction
    (D) immorality (E) lack of rules

14. **contend** (A) oppose (B) agree with (C) be serene (D) scorn (E) laugh

15. **ideology** (A) false religion (B) set of beliefs (C) false prophecy
    (D) carving in stone (E) superstition

16. **chauvinist** (A) traitor (B) exhibitionist (C) countryman (D) extreme patriot
    (E) actor

17. **meticulous** (A) fastidious (B) careless (C) measured (D) expressive
    (E) deliberate

18. **salient** (A) salty (B) indiscernible (C) flighty (D) lucrative (E) prominent

19. **proctor**   (A) gambler   (B) medical specialist   (C) supervisor   (D) practitioner
(E) helper

20. **inadvertence**   (A) lacking in difficulty   (B) intentional action   (C) poor choice
(D) unwittingness   (E) inconsideration

21. **concur**   (A) confuse   (B) agree   (C) shock   (D) happen at the same time
(E) be similar

22. **retract**   (A) take back   (B) deny   (C) go over again   (D) re-measure
(E) testify again

23. **temperament**   (A) patience   (B) emotional instability   (C) disposition
(D) lacking in anger   (E) moderation

24. **peer**   (A) commoner   (B) classmate   (C) pressure group   (D) equal   (E) nobleman

25. **flagrant**   (A) overt   (B) sweet-smelling   (C) flammable   (D) punitive   (E) firm

26. **erudition**   (A) ignorance   (B) conceit   (C) obliteration   (D) pedantry   (E) learning

PRACTICE SET 14
ANSWER KEY

1. B
2. C
3. E
4. B
5. D
6. B
7. A
8. C
9. B
10. E
11. E
12. A
13. C
14. A
15. B
16. D
17. A
18. E
19. C
20. D
21. B
22. A
23. C
24. D
25. A
26. E

CHARADE   a pretense (n)

Synonyms:

Antonyms:

Context: The candidate complained that the investigating committee's questions were merely a political **charade**.

Self-Referential:

HALLMARK   distinguishing mark (n)

Synonyms:

Antonyms:

Context: Constant references to patriotism were a **hallmark** of the candidate's speeches.

Self-Referential:

VESTIGE   a remnant, a trace (n)

Synonyms:

Antonyms:

Context: The appendix is said to be a **vestige** of a second stomach in the anatomy of ancient humans.

Self-Referential:

TAPESTRY   a decorative wall hanging (n)

Synonyms:

Antonyms:

Context: The walls of ancient castles were often hung with **tapestries** depicting great battles.

Self-Referential:

VERNACULAR   common speech, ordinary language (n)

Synonyms:

Antonyms:

Context: The most difficult problem in learning a language is to become familiar with the **vernacular** of rural regions.

Self-Referential:

CONCISE exact (adj)

Synonyms:

Antonyms:

Context: It is difficult to come up with a **concise** definition of the word ethics.

Self-Referential:

TERSE short, curt (adj)

Synonyms:

Antonyms:

Context: The angry judge delivered the verdict in short, **terse** sentences.

Self-Referential:

CIRCUITOUS round-about, indirect (adj)

Synonyms:

Antonyms:

Context: Railroad travel from Texas to South Carolina involves a very **circuitous** route.

Self-Referential:

SUPERFLUITY excess (n)

Synonyms:

Antonyms:

Context: The critic noted that the book was marred by a **superfluity** of trite observations.

Self-Referential:

VERBIAGE   excessive wordiness (n)

Synonyms:

Antonyms:

Context: The readers of Marcel's new book will be assaulted by the contrived **verbiage** of his prose.

Self-Referential:

GREGARIOUS   outgoing, very friendly (adj)

Synonyms:

Antonyms:

Context: An office seeker is sometimes cautioned that it is dangerous to be too **gregarious**.

Self-Referential:

LOQUACIOUS   extremely talkative and articulate (adj)

Synonyms:

Antonyms:

Context: A **loquacious** guest can sway the opinions of a party of ignoramuses.

Self-Referential:

PRATE   to chatter, to talk meaninglessly (v)

Synonyms:

Antonyms:

Context: The team was tired of hearing Jones **prate** of his athletic prowess.

Self-Referential:

VOLUBLE   fluent, talkative (adj)

Synonyms:

Antonyms:

Context: The legislature is often filled with **voluble** expressions of absurd opinion.

Self-Referential:

DISCOURSE   conversation, a long paper or speech on a subject (n)

Synonyms:

Antonyms:

Context: The dean prepared to give a **discourse** on the proper governing of a university.

Self-Referential:

RUNIC   like runes, mysterious, secret (adj)

Synonyms:

Antonyms:

Context: The caves of the ancient tribes were covered with **runic** decorations and drawings.

Self-Referential:

RETICENT   not talkative (adj)

Synonyms:

Antonyms:

Context: The student was extremely **reticent** about taking credit for the paper that his friend wrote for him.

Self-Referential:

CRYPTIC   encoded, secret, indecipherable (adj)

Synonyms:

Antonyms:

Context: Many scholars believe that the author makes **cryptic** references to historical figures.

Self-Referential:

ESOTERIC   hidden, available only to the initiate (adj)

Synonyms:

Antonyms:

Context: The religious initiate was proud that he had been admitted to such an **esoteric** fellowship

Self-Referential:

ECLIPSE   overshadowing, esp. of the sun or moon (n)

Synonyms:

Antonyms:

Context: The protagonist's knowledge of a coming **eclipse** saved him from death in Mark Twain's *A Connecticut Yankee in King Arthur's Court.*

Self-Referential:

LATENT   potential, hidden quality (adj)

Synonyms:

Antonyms:

Context: Grandma Moses was unaware of her **latent** talent as an artist until she was in her eighties.

Self-Referential:

APOCRYPHAL   spurious, not genuine (adj)

Synonyms:

Antonyms:

Context: The story of George Washington and the cherry tree is **apocryphal** at best.

Self-Referential:

DISSEMBLE   to lie (v)

Synonyms:

Antonyms:

Context: George Washington claimed that he was unable to **dissemble**.

Self-Referential:

PREVARICATE   to lie (v)

Synonyms:

Antonyms:

Context: If George Washington had **prevaricated** regarding his actions toward the cherry tree, he may never have become president.

Self-Referential:

SIMULATE   to imitate, to make seem real (v)

Synonyms:

Antonyms:

Context: Many food companies have tried to **simulate** sugar, but with limited success.

Self-Referential:

HYPERBOLE   excessive exaggeration (n)

Synonyms:

Antonyms:

Context: Many southern storytellers use **hyperbole** as a literary device, especially in the tall tales of Staggerlee or High John the Conqueror.

Self-Referential:

PRACTICE SET 15

Instructions: Circle the answer that most closely approximates the definition of the word given.

1. **hallmark**   (A) designated room   (B) imaginary sign   (C) remnant
   (D) distinguishing mark   (E) wall decoration

2. **runic**   (A) competitive   (B) mysterious   (C) in disrepair   (D) obvious   (E) stunted

3. **esoteric**   (A) secret   (B) learned   (C) well-known   (D) high-flown   (E) plain

4. **verbiage**   (A) rubbish   (B) few words   (C) excessive verbs   (D) swearing
   (E) excessive wordiness

5. **tapestry**   (A) barroom   (B) bandaging   (C) wall hanging   (D) framed painting
   (E) rhythmical pattern

6. **concise**   (A) indirect   (B) exact   (C) conceited   (D) unnecessary   (E) beclouded

7. **voluble**   (A) talkative   (B) loud   (C) precious   (D) resilient   (E) massive

8. **circuitous**   (A) direct   (B) curious   (C) roundabout   (D) as a carnival
   (E) unquestionable

9. **vestige**   (A) remnant   (B) apparel   (C) worship service   (D) church committee
   (E) gamble

10. **terse**   (A) true   (B) tantalizing   (C) drawn out   (D) written   (E) short

11. **charade**   (A) procession   (B) shaving   (C) narrow crack   (D) pretense
    (E) cautious display

12. **cryptic**   (A) vaulted   (B) crossed   (C) in code   (D) underground   (E) open

13. **discourse**   (A) informal chat   (B) conversation   (C) rudeness   (D) discovery
    (E) rambling journey

14. **vernacular**   (A) intestine   (B) erudite language   (C) profanity   (D) common speech
    (E) expletive

15. **simulate**   (A) inspire   (B) satirize   (C) sparkle   (D) reverse   (E) imitate

16. **latent**   (A) potential   (B) rubber-like   (C) swimming   (D) kinetic   (E) unexpected

17. **apocryphal**   (A) lying   (B) of dubious authenticity   (C) revelatory   (D) certain
    (E) dark

18. **reticent**   (A) odorous   (B) near past   (C) reluctant to talk   (D) limited   (E) slow

19. **dissemble**   (A) take apart   (B) show a difference   (C) tell the truth   (D) lie
    (E) tease

20. **superfluity** (A) uselessness (B) face value (C) excess (D) frugality (E) superiority

21. **hyperbole** (A) unproved theory (B) exaggeration (C) extreme agitation (D) publicity (E) oversight

22. **prevaricate** (A) prepare ahead (B) imitate (C) lie (D) blurt out (E) surprise

23. **eclipse** (A) overshadowing (B) revelation (C) collapse (D) public speech (E) dishonest ploy

24. **gregarious** (A) ecclesiastical (B) isolated (C) friendly (D) shy (E) greedy

25. **prate** (A) pack (B) babble (C) price (D) weigh (E) assess

26. **loquacious** (A) nearby (B) talkative (C) roundabout (D) local (E) linked

158

PRACTICE SET 15
ANSWER KEY

1. D
2. B
3. A
4. E
5. C
6. B
7. A
8. C
9. A
10. E
11. D
12. C
13. B
14. D
15. E
16. A
17. B
18. C
19. D
20. C
21. B
22. C
23. A
24. C
25. B
26. B

TOUT   to solicit or promote (v)

Synonyms:

Antonyms:

Context: In his last days the philosopher George Berkeley spent much time
                            touting tar water as a panacea.

Self-Referential:

SEINE   a fishnet (n)

Synonyms:

Antonyms:

Context: In regions where fish are plentiful, **seine** fishing is the usual method.

Self-Referential:

AMENABLE   agreeable, obedient (adj)

Synonyms:

Antonyms:

Context: I am **amenable** to any arrangement you may make.

Self-Referential:

DIFFIDENT   shy, reserved (adj)

Synonyms:

Antonyms:

Context: A psychiatrist will always have trouble analyzing a patient's problem when the patient is excessively **diffident**.

Self-Referential:

ADAMANT   hard, unyielding, **or** a very hard stone (adj, n)

Synonyms:

Antonyms:

Context: The father was **adamant** in his refusal to let his son use the family car.

The objects found in the burial site were made of **adamant**, showing a high degree of craftsmanship.

Self-Referential:

IMPLACABLE   not able to be changed (adj)

Synonyms:

Antonyms:

Context: Despite protests from the union, the school principal was **implacable** regarding her decision to fire the worst teachers.

Self-Referential:

INTRANSIGENT   stubborn, uncompromising (adj)

Synonyms:

Antonyms:

Context: Yeats could not win Maude Gonne's hand in marriage because she was too **intransigent**.

Self-Referential:

OBSTINATE   stubborn, unmoving (adj)

Synonyms:

Antonyms:

Context: The horse was **obstinate** in its refusal to cross the grating.

Self-Referential:

AMBIVALENT   uncertain, having conflicting feelings (adj)

Synonyms:

Antonyms:

Context: I am **ambivalent** in my feelings about tax reform; there are too many problems involved.

Self-Referential:

FLUCTUATE   to vary widely (v)

Synonyms:

Antonyms:

Context: My blood pressure is not steady; it **fluctuates** from day to day.

Self-Referential:

CAPRICE   impulsive action, whim (n)

Synonyms:

Antonyms:

Context: His decision to give away all his money was the product of a mere **caprice**.

Self-Referential:

FICKLE   changeable, not constant (adj)

Synonyms:

Antonyms:

Context: Larry was altogether **fickle**; his actions from day to day were entirely contradictory.

Self-Referential:

IMPROMPTU   spontaneous, spur of the moment (adj)

Synonyms:

Antonyms:

Context: Frost's poem, "Stopping by Woods on a Snowy Evening," was an **impromptu** creation.

Self-Referential:

ABSCOND to run away secretly (v)

Synonyms:

Antonyms:

Context: The author's hopes of publication were dashed when one of the publisher's employees **absconded** with the funds.

Self-Referential:

ELUSIVE difficult to find or pin down (adj)

Synonyms:

Antonyms:

Context: There is an **elusive** quality about Schubert's music that puzzles critics.

Self-Referential:

PARRY to fend off, dodge (v)

Synonyms:

Antonyms:

Context: The real joy in listening to debates is in hearing the opponents **parry** each other's attacks.

Self-Referential:

SHIRK to neglect or ignore (v)

Synonyms:

Antonyms:

Context: When one **shirks** his responsibilities, he robs another of his freedom.

Self-Referential:

ASPIRATION   hope, ambition, **or** breathing in (n)

Synonyms:

Antonyms:

Context: My **aspiration** to earn my living as a musician has never been fulfilled.

My **aspiration** to earn my living as a musician has never been fulfilled.

Her **aspiration** was impeded by a blocked windpipe.

Self-Referential:

AVARICE   greed (n)

Synonyms:

Antonyms:

Context: **Avarice** is the major cause of criminal behavior.

Self-Referential:

PROCLIVITY   tendency (n)

Synonyms:

Antonyms:

Context: I have an enormous **proclivity** for postponing decisions.

Self-Referential:

PREDESTINE   to determine ahead of time (v)

Synonyms:

Antonyms:

Context: Her refusal to prepare for the event **predestined** her for failure.

Self-Referential:

INSTIGATE to urge, incite (v)

Synonyms:

Antonyms:

Context: By his inflammatory actions, he **instigated** a riot in his community.

Self-Referential:

INVEIGLE to acquire through sneakiness (v)

Synonyms:

Antonyms:

Context: Through his dishonest dealings, he **inveigled** an illegal transfer of money to his account.

Self-Referential:

PIQUANT spicy, as in hot sauce, **or** stimulating, provocative (adj)

Synonyms:

Antonyms:

Context: The chicken breast was served in a **piquant** sauce on a bed of spanish rice.
Molly is a **piquant** speaker; her words always rile people.

Self-Referential:

TANTALIZE to tease, give a taste of (v)

Synonyms:

Antonyms:

Context: You never fulfill your promises; you merely **tantalize** me with your suggestions.

Self-Referential:

PROFUSE   plentiful (adj)

Synonyms:

Antonyms:

Context: The **profuse** strains of the mockingbird's songs are joyful and mysterious.

Self-Referential:

PRACTICE SET 16

Instructions: Circle the answer that most closely approximates the definition of the word given.

1. **tout** (A) play down (B) promote (C) tow (D) obscure (E) sound a horn

2. **adamant** (A) earthy (B) original (C) firm (D) easily persuaded (E) waffling

3. **avarice** (A) goodness (B) opposition (C) confession (D) epitome (E) greed

4. **tantalize** (A) soothe (B) tease (C) pour liquids (D) intertwine (E) misrepresent

5. **fickle** (A) changeable (B) irresponsible (C) not factually true (D) nervous
   (E) trustworthy

6. **seine** (A) coil of thread (B) weight (C) hook (D) fishnet (E) seed

7. **implacable** (A) tractable (B) not changeable (C) unpleasant (D) changeable
   (E) improving

8. **proclivity** (A) slope (B) steepness (C) inclination (D) favor (E) habitual error

9. **profuse** (A) plentiful (B) disparate (C) simple (D) lean (E) many-leaved

10. **impromptu** (A) unhurried (B) tardy (C) impolite (D) spontaneous
    (E) impractical

11. **amenable** (A) correctable (B) friendly (C) agreeable (D) forgetful
    (E) forgivable

12. **intransigent** (A) traveling (B) stubborn (C) nearly invisible (D) vacillating
    (E) fearless

13. **predestine** (A) condemn (B) doom (C) project (D) determine in advance
    (E) decide later

14. **abscond** (A) refrain (B) abbreviate (C) shorten (D) leave secretly (E) scrape

15. **diffident** (A) reserved (B) brazen (C) hard to understand (D) refracting light
    (E) spreading

16. **obstinate** (A) no longer current (B) stubborn (C) blocked
    (D) inclined to abstention (E) acceptable

17. **instigate** (A) examine in detail (B) combine (C) incite (D) question (E) present

18. **elusive** (A) referential (B) escaping (C) drawn forth (D) easy to find
    (E) difficult to pinpoint

19. **ambivalent** (A) confusing (B) double entendre (C) clear (D) moving about
    (E) uncertain

20. **inveigle**   (A) deceive   (B) attack   (C) acquire by sneakiness   (D) discover by spying
(E) enter with vigor

21. **parry**   (A) act   (B) ward off   (C) halt   (D) repeat   (E) pass on

22. **fluctuate**   (A) flow   (B) channel directly   (C) change regularly   (D) confuse
(E) vary widely

23. **piquant**   (A) angry   (B) near the top   (C) enthusiastic   (D) stimulating   (E) bland

24. **shirk**   (A) reduce   (B) concentrate   (C) neglect   (D) shift   (E) gather

25. **caprice**   (A) soft hat   (B) whim   (C) projection of land   (D) concerto   (E) wealth

26. **aspiration**   (A) hope   (B) circular breathing   (C) stimulation   (D) hopelessness
(E) implication

PRACTICE SET 16
ANSWER KEY

1. B
2. C
3. E
4. B
5. A
6. D
7. B
8. C
9. A
10. D
11. C
12. B
13. D
14. D
15. A
16. B
17. C
18. E
19. E
20. C
21. B
22. E
23. D
24. C
25. B
26. A

Supplementary Word List

You have now completed your review of those vocabulary words we consider *essential* for an outstanding performance on your test. If you have additional study time available, we recommend that you make your own exercises for unfamiliar words from the following list. You may photocopy page 175 for your exercises. Also use page 175 for any new words that you encounter while reading.

abate
abeyance
abhor
abject
abrogate
absolve
abstemious
abstruse
abysmal
acclimate
accolade
accretion
acerbity
acme
acquiescence
acrimonious
acumen
adage
admonish
adroit
advert
aegis
affectation
affidavit
affinity
agenda
agnostic
agrarian
alias
allegory
alleviate
alliteration
allusion
altercation
amazon
ambiguous
ameliorate
amoral
amortization
anagram
analogy
analysis
anathema
animadversion

animosity
animus
annotate
antediluvian
anthology
anthropology
anticlimax
antonym
apathetic
aphorism
apotheosis
appellation
appendage
apportion
apprise
apropos
apt
arable
arbiter
archaic
archives
arraign
arrears
artifice
askance
asperity
assiduous
assimilate
assuage
asterisk
atavism
atheist
atrophy
attenuate
attrition
augury
auspicious
austerity
automation
autonomous
avid
avocation
awry
axiom

bagatelle
banal
bathos
bayou
belles-lettres
bellicose
belligerent
bellwether
benevolent
benignant
bereavement
bestial
billingsgate
bizarre
blasé
blasphemy
blatant
bonanza
boorish
bowdlerize
broach
buoyant
bureaucracy
burgeoning

cabal
cache
cacophony
cadaver
cajole
calumny
canard
capital
carnivorous
carping
cataclysm
catechism
cathartic
caucus
celestial
censure
centaur
centrifugal

cerebral
chameleon
charlatan
chimera
chronological
circumspect
circumvent
clandestine
cleavage
cliché
coercion
cogent
cognizant
cognomen
colloquial
collusion
comity
commiserate
compendium
complacent
complaisant
compunction
conative
concave
concentric
concomitant
concrete
condone
conduit
congenial
congenital
conjecture
connotation
context
contingency
contretemps
contravene
contumacious
convivial
copious
corollary
corporeal
corpulent
correlation
cosset
coterie
covert
cozen
crass
credence
credible
creditable
creditor
credo

credulity
credulous
crescent
criterion
crux
cupidity
curator
cursory
cynosure
debacle
debenture
debilitating
debit
decimate
décolleté
decor
decorum
deductive
defection
deleterious
demagogue
denotation
denouement
deprecate
derogatory
desiccate
desideratum
desultory
devious
dexterous
diatribe
diction
didactic
dido
dilatory
discomfort
discursive
dishabille
disparage
disparity
dispassionate
dissimulation
dissonant
distaff
dolorous
duplicity
duress

ecclesiastical
éclat
effete
effluvium
egoist
egotist

egregious
eleemosynary
emanate
emeritus
emolument
empirical
emulate
enclave
encomium
enervate
enigma
enjoin
enmity
ennui
enormity
entomology
entrepreneur
epicurean
epigram
epithet
epitome
equanimity
equine
equitable
equity
equivocate
esthetic
ethics
ethnic
etymology
eugenics
eulogy
evanescent
excoriate
execrable
exegesis
exhortation
exhume
ex officio
exercise
exotic
expatiate
expedite
expiate
extant
extenuating
extirpate
extradite
extraneous
extrovert
facet
facetious
facile
fallible

fastidious	imperturbable	inundate
feasible	impervious	invalidate
fecund	implementation	invective
fester	imply	inveigh
fetish	importune	inveterate
fetters	impotent	invidious
fiduciary	impregnable	inviolate
figurative	improvident	invoice
foible	impugn	irascible
foreclosure	incarcerate	irony
formidable	incarnation	irrelevant
forte	inchoate	irrevocable
fortuitous	incisive	itinerary
fulcrum	incognito	
	incongruous	jeremiad
gamut	incorrigible	jingo
garnishee	incredible	journeyman
gaucherie	incredulity	judicious
genealogy	incredulous	juncture
generic	increment	jurisprudence
genre	incriminate	juxtaposition
genuflect	inculcate	
germane	incumbent	kaleidoscope
gestation	indigent	
gesticulate	indolent	lachrymose
glossary	inductive	larceny
graphic	indulgent	largess
grimace	ineffable	laudable
	inept	lecherous
hackneyed	inertia	legacy
harbinger	inexorable	lethargy
heinous	infallible	lexicon
hiatus	infer	libel
hirsute	ingenue	libido
histrionic	ingratiate	libretto
holocaust	inimical	litany
homogeneous	iniquitous	literal
humility	innate	literati
husbandry	innocuous	litigation
hybrid	innuendo	lucrative
	inorganic	lugubrious
iconoclast	insatiable	luxuriant
idiom	inscrutable	lyric
idiosyncrasy	insidious	
ignominious	insipid	macadam
illusive	insolvent	machinations
imagery	insouciance	maelstrom
imbibe	insular	magnanimous
imminent	integral	maladroit
immolation	intelligentsia	malapropism
impasse	interim	malcontent
impassive	internecine	malefactor
impeach	intimidate	malign
impeccable	introvert	malignant

malingerer
mammal
man date
mandatory
mania
manifest
manifesto
mastiff
maudlin
mauve
maxim
mayhem
meander
median
mediator
melee
mendacity
mentor
mercurial
meretricious
mesa
mesmerize
metaphor
metaphysical
miasma
microcosm
milieu
militant
millennium
minutiae
misapprehension
miscreant
misogynist
mitigate
modicum
momentum
moor
moratorium
morbid
moribund
motley
mugwump
mulch
munificent
mutable
mutual
myopic
myriad
mystic

naive
nascent
natal
nebulous

necromancy
nefarious
negotiable
nemesis
nomad
nonchalant
nosegay
nostalgia
noxious
nucleus

obeisance
obfuscation
obsolete
obstetrician
obstreperous
occidental
occult
odious
odium
officious
olfactory
oligarchy
ominous
omnipotent
omnipresent
omniscient
omnivorous
onerous
onus
opportunist
opprobrium
optimism
option
opus
orgy
ornithology
orthography
ostracize
oxidation

paddock
paean
palatable
palliate
palpable
panacea
panache
panegyric
panoply
parable
paramour
paranoia
parapet

paraphrase
parasite
parish
parity
parochial
parody
parsimonious
passé
passive
pathological
pathos
patriarch
patrimony
paucity
pecuniary
pedagogue
pediment
penchant
penitent
pensive
penultimate
penurious
perdition
peregrination
peremptory
perennial
perfidious
perfunctory
peripatetic
periphery
perjury
pernicious
peroration
perquisite
persiflage
perspective
perverse
petulant
pharisaical
philology
phlegmatic
phobia
physiognomy
physiological
plagiarize
platonic
plausible
plebeian
plebiscite
plenary
poignant
polemic
polyglot
portentous

posthumous
potpourri
pragmatic
precedence
precept
précis
precocious
predatory
predilection
preempt
preponderance
prerogative
presage
prescience
prevarication
primogeniture
pristine
procrastinate
proficient
prognosticate
proletarian
prolific
prolix
promulgate
propagate
propinquity
propitious
proponent
prosaic
proscenium
proselytize
protagonist
protégé
protocol
prototype
provincial
proximity
proxy
pseudonym
psyche
psychiatry
psychopathic
psychosis
puerile
punctilious
purview
pusillanimous

quadruped
quandary
quarantine
querulous
quietus
quintessence

rabid
ramification
rampart
rancor
rapacious
rapprochement
ratiocination
rational
rationalize
reactionary
recondite
recrimination
refurbish
regimen
relegate
relevant
remonstrate
renaissance
rendezvous
repartee
repertoire
replete
reprehensible
rescind
residue
resilient
respite
restive
resurgence
retrospective
reverie
revile
ribald
robot
rococo
rostrum
rotunda
ruminate
rustic
rusticate

sacrilegious
sacrosanct
sadism
salubrious
salutary
sanguine
sarcasm
sardonic
sartorial
satiate
satire
saturnine

satyr
savant
schism
scion
scrutiny
scurrilous
secular
sedentary
sedulous
semantics
senile
sensory
sensual
sensuous
sententious
sepulcher
sequester
seraph
serendipity
servile
simile
similitude
simony
sinecure
skeptic
slander
smug
sobriety
sobriquet
soliloquy
soluble
somnambulist
somnolent
sonorous
sophist
sophisticated
soporific
spasmodic
spontaneity
spoonerism
squeamish
staccato
staid
stamina
status
statutory
stealth
stigma
stilted
stipend
stoic
stolid
stratagem
strategic

stratum
stricture
strident
stultify
suave
sublimate
subsidy
substantive
subterfuge
supercilious
superficial
superimpose
supernal
supine
surcease
surfeit
surname
surreptitious
surveillance
sycophant
syllogism
symmetry

taciturn
talisman
tangible
tautology
tawdry
temerity
temporal
tenable
tenet
tenure
termagant
testator
therapeutic
thwart
titular
tome
torpid
torturous
toxic
transpire
trenchant
trepidation
trilogy
trite
turgid
tyro

unconscionable
unctuous
undulation
unilateral

untenable
usurp
usury
utopia
uxorious

vacillate
vagary
valedictory
valid
vehement
venal
venerable
venery
venial
verbatim
verbose
vernal
vicarious
vicissitude
vindicate
virulent
vitiate
vitriolic
vivisection
vociferous
volition
vulnerable

warranty

zenith

Synonyms:

Antonyms:

Context:

Self-Referential:

Synonyms:

Antonyms:

Context:

Self-Referential:

Synonyms:

Antonyms:

Context:

Self-Referential:

Synonyms:

Antonyms:

Context:

Self-Referential:

Synonyms:

Antonyms:

Context:

Self-Referential: